THE SPIRITUAL HISTORY OF THE DEAD SEA SECT

David Flusser

THE SPIRITUAL HISTORY OF THE DEAD SEA SECT

MOD Books   Tel-Aviv

THE SPIRITUAL HISTORY OF THE DEAD SEA SECT
by
DAVID FLUSSER

English translation by Carol Glucker

English Series Editor: Shmuel Himelstein

ISBN 965-05-0480-X

Computerized phototypesetting & printing: Naidat Press Ltd.
Printed in Israel

MOD Books — P.O.B. 7103, Tel-Aviv 61070, ISRAEL

Contents

PREFACE

Before you, dear reader, are lectures which I delivered in the Broadcast University of the Israel Defense Forces Radio. In preparing them for print, I tried, as far as possible, not to alter the style of the lectures, in order to preserve the living spirit of the spoken word. I have also retained the structure of the lectures. But at the same time I have made many corrections, and even additions, to complete the picture. Most of the quotations from the Dead Sea Scrolls are cited in the notes, and there I have added a large number of references. The notes are an essential part of the work.

I know that the language of the scrolls is not identical to that of modern Hebrew. That is not only because of the distance in time, but because the Essenes developed a special, to some extent artificial, language. The modern Hebrew reader who wishes to verify the sources in the original (they are given in English translation in the footnotes), has to become accustomed to this strange language in order to get the most out of the passages I have quoted.

Today the scrolls are well-known to the Israeli public as a sensational discovery and as an archaeological treasure which flatters our national pride, while knowledge about the nature and the beliefs of the Dead Sea Sect, which scholars rightly identify with the Essenes, is gradually declining. This phenomenon also characterizes international scholarly research, which increasingly deals with details and neglects the wider picture. I have tried to paint this picture here, relying on both the work of other scholars and on my own research, and I hope the reader will benefit from it.

The Essene sect was one of the strangest phenomena in Jewish history, and in the history of all mankind. I have concentrated on describing the general picture, while touching on the influence of Essene thought on the world only when the subject called for it. My main intention was to introduce the reader to the Essenes themselves, so that he can tackle the challenge of Essene ideology in the light of his own beliefs. If I have succeeded in this task, perhaps this extraordinary meeting with these followers of a profound and clear-cut system of thought will be a fruitful one.

If the reader finds Essene thought limited, perhaps he will discover that his own beliefs also have limitations and unsubstantiated assumptions, and that his own philosophy and expectations, like those of the Essenes, are also "castles in the air." At any rate, it is worthwhile for the modern reader to ask himself whether he himself, like the Essenes, is not yearning for a better world, whether he thinks it a bad thing to "abstain from all evil, and hold fast to all good, that they may practice truth, righteousness and justice upon earth" (*The Community Rule* 1:4-6).

Even before the discovery of the scrolls, we knew that the Essenes hoped for a better world and a more elevated social order, and the scrolls have confirmed that this was their outlook. I have not concealed the darker side of Essene ideology, but it is nevertheless only right that we should rather look at the light of these Sons of Light.

Many people are accustomed to travelling to distant lands, to get to know other people and other cultures. I have tried in my lectures and in this book, which includes the lectures, to be a kind of guide on a journey into the Jewish past. I hope that this trip to see the Essenes proves worthwhile, and that I have not been too bad a guide.

Prof. David Flusser

I.

The Essenes and their Origins

In the following chapters we will discuss one of the most important and fascinating discoveries of modern times, the way of life and thought of the sect whose writings were discovered at Qumran. This was a very interesting sect with a very particular view of the world, which expressed for the first time ideas of the utmost importance to this very day. The great discovery in 1947 and subsequent findings brought about a revolution in the history of human thought. We will try to examine and understand the members of this sect as if we were among them, and will try to see what we can learn from them. The people of the scrolls were among the most interesting phenomena in the history of Israel in the Second Temple period, and it may even be possible to learn from them something toward solving the eternal problems that confront mankind in general, and in particular the People of Israel residing in Zion.

Complete scrolls and fragments of scrolls were found in caves near Qumran. A large number of these scrolls have already been published and one can learn from them, but some have not yet been published, and there are fragments which perhaps only our children will be fortunate enough to see. But we have already gained a clear picture of a particular Jewish sect, which grew out of a broader spiritual movement which looked forward to the end and to redemption, a sect which loved to write and to collect books. We will leave the discussion of the Biblical books found among the scrolls to scholars of Biblical criticism; Biblical texts were found that are hundreds of years older than the versions of these books we have today. We will discuss them only when they touch upon our subject. Fragments of apocryphal books were also found, some already published, which make it possible for us to look further back, to the Persian period, like the well-known *Book of Tobit*, or a section from *Ben Sira* (*Ecclesiasticus*). We will discuss here only those writings which represent the broad ideological stream from which this sect, the Sect of the Scrolls, emerged.

In fact we already had some information about the Sect of the Scrolls in the writings of ancient authors. The first discoverers of the scrolls, particularly Prof. Sukenik, who was the very first, realized that this Sect of the Scrolls was the Essene sect.

We had already known about the Essenes before the discovery of the scrolls, from the works of ancient writers.[1] The most important source is the works of Flavius Josephus, who wrote in Greek. Another source is the writings of the renowned Jewish philosopher, Philo of Alexandria, also in Greek. Apart from them, a reference is preserved in a Greek writer named Dio Chrysostom, who lived in the first and second centuries C.E. He says that the Essenes comprised an entire prosperous city beside the Dead Sea. The Essene settlement is also mentioned by another Gentile writer, Pliny the Elder, who lived in the first century C.E. and wrote in Latin; his enormous work deals with natural history.

The name "Essenes" does not appear in the new scrolls. In the Greek sources they are called *Essaioi* (*Essaei* in Latin), or *Essenoi* (*Esseni* in Latin).[2] The Hebrew form *Isi'im* has no basis in early sources. It is derived from the fact that an Italian Jewish scholar named Azariah dei Rossi transcribed the Latin name *Essaei* into the word *Isi'i* in his book *Ma'or Einayim* (1575). From the ancient period down to the present day there have been numerous conjectures as to the meaning of the name "Essenes." More than a thousand years, ago the author of the Hebrew work *Josippon* thought that the Latin form of the name was a transcription of the Hebrew *hasidim* ("pious ones"). Others thought that the name was the Aramaic word *asia* (a physician). The whole question is, however, not very important to the main issue.

Although in the past we have had the information about the Essenes passed down to us by ancient authors, it is only now, when we possess their writings, that we can see what they were really like. We know about the Sadducees, for example, only from their opponents, and we have no direct information on them, while as far as the Essenes are concerned, we have not only sympathetic descriptions in the works of ancient authors, but also their own writings, the scrolls. Today the scrolls illuminate the ancient authors' accounts of the Essenes, so that it is possible to write a commentary on Josephus' description of the Essenes from the scrolls themselves.

If the information from ancient authors is combined with that from the scrolls, even their history can be studied. Among the scrolls are found works which are certainly related and linked to Essene writings, but are not themselves entirely Essene. Presumably, therefore, Essenism grew out of a broader movement. The Essenes themselves were people occupied with meditations on the ultimate mystery of God, who studied the Bible in order to find in it their place in the history of the world. They also composed their own works of biblical exegesis, and organized what is, in fact, the earliest "communistic" society known to us. They settled in the Dead Sea area, close to Ein Gedi, and put their scrolls in the caves, exactly in the places where they were found.

Perhaps it is worth mentioning that there was another group of Essenes, or semi-Essenes, who lived near Damascus and whose writings were already known from the Cairo Genizah. The work found in the Genizah is known to scholars as the *Damascus Rule*. (The Cairo Genizah is a collection of ancient documents copied in the Middle Ages.) This work was known for a long time before the scrolls were found, but it was not known exactly how it should be understood. It was, again, the late Prof. Sukenik who discovered the connection between the group that settled near Damascus and the Essenes. Eventually, his findings were confirmed by the discovery at Qumran as well of fragments of the same *Damascus Rule*, but only some of these have yet been published. The group living near

Damascus was less exclusive than the one which lived beside the Dead Sea.

The assumption that the Sect of the Scrolls was actually the Essenes was not accepted immediately. There were scholars who wanted to identify the Sect of the Scrolls, the *Yahad* (Community) as they called themselves, with different Jewish groups of the same period. There were even scholars who regarded the scrolls as Christian compositions, something which is quite impossible, since there is nothing Christian in them. But absence of evidence is, of course, no proof.

Other scholars, because of a certain similarity in methods of organization between the Essene community and the Pharisee community, wanted to identify them with the Pharisees. But this is impossible, because of their particular *halakhah*. Even their special solar calendar was different from the normal Jewish calendar. There were also those who wanted to identify them with the Zealots, a most improbable identification, because of their particular, isolationist attitude to the rest of the Jewish people, and because of their pacifist tendency.

Essene Isolationism

On the other hand, it is possible to prove, without any doubt, their identification with the Essenes of Josephus, of Philo of Alexandria and of Pliny. In particular, if one reads the words of Josephus, the elements which are common to both illuminate each other; Josephus illuminates the scrolls and the scrolls Josephus. The place of the sect in society, its organization and its ideas are the ideas of an isolationist group, which developed a concrete view of the world, a kind of closed way of thinking. The extremism they adopted was what enabled them to regard the problems of the world in a manner which was clear-cut and one-sided, and this makes it most interesting and instructive. Sometimes extremism, reductionism, and even a certain amount of distortion can illuminate some issues about God and the Jewish people in a very particular light.

We have before us a sect so separatist that Josephus finds it worth making specific note that it was of Jewish origin. Its members were very different from other Jews, and yet their ideas were based on concepts common to all streams existing in the Second Temple period; common ideas of how to understand the Bible by way of midrash, of the expectation of the End of Days, and of the concept of the Chosen People. But on this last point the Essenes were different from the rest of the Jewish people, in that they saw themselves as "Israel that walks in the way of perfection," as the "true Israel." (Later, following in their footsteps, the Christian Church regarded itself as the "true Israel.") Facing the Essenes was a serious problem: What should be the correct attitude toward the rest of the Jewish people? Would God condemn everyone else to destruction, or would the majority of the Jewish people accept the Essenes' sovereignty at the last moment? The group's isolationism was one of the most interesting phenomena about it. It proclaimed the idea of election. Just as in the past, not all of Israel had been saved and some people had died in the desert, and just as only the Kingdom of Judah had survived and not the Ten Tribes, there was a continuing process of winnowing and election toward the Essenes themselves. Thus, on the one hand, they had to preserve their isolation, and on the other hand, to develop the hope that the majority of the Jewish people would join them at the End of Days.[3] In other words, it was a particular attitude of a closed society, whose members, living within it, developed their own particular ideas and social arrangements. These people created an isolationist and united society.

In the Second Temple period various groups arose, each of which saw itself as representing the Kingdom of Heaven and the people of Israel, "a kingdom of priests, and a holy nation," and a certain tendency to think of themselves as an elite grew up among these groups; many of them believed that only they represented Israel. This process also gave rise to the Pharisees and the Hasidim, who called themselves "the Congregation of the Pious." These groups felt that they were the elite of the Jewish people, but the Essenes went one step further and saw themselves as *the* Jewish people, the chosen, the elect, in whose footsteps the rest should follow, or else

13

incur everlasting perdition. This approach gave rise to the communal social framework involving isolation from "the assemblies of men of evil," going to the desert and abandoning the dwellings of men and, apparently at a later stage, founding separate Essene cells within towns, as Josephus tells us.

Their isolationism aroused tension within them: between their attitude to the Temple and their hope of wresting the people of Israel and the whole Land of Israel from the hands of its enemies. Following this, tension was generated between them and the rest of the Jews (not only in Eretz Israel, but also abroad). They did, however, have an immense power of attraction.

In Cave No. 7 only Greek fragments were found, but unfortunately very small ones. These fragments must have been of books placed in this cave by those Jews from the Greek Diaspora who joined the Essenes, lived among them and learned from them. It was evidently from these Jews that Essene ideas spread throughout the entire world. According to Josephus (*Jewish War* II, 154-185), the promise the Essenes gave people that those who would join them would earn everlasting life, life in Paradise, that their souls would reach the true Garden of Eden, attracted many people.

An additional, very strange paradox is involved here: this group, which forbade the acceptance of gifts without the permission of those in authority (see Josephus, *Jewish War* II:134), whose doctrines were so secret that it wrote certain things in code, this sect which ordained hatred toward others as a religious commandment and at the same time created a closed society — was precisely the group which earned widespread fame throughout the Jewish and the non-Jewish world, and everyone who wrote about it did so with admiration. Apparently, travellers who visited Eretz Israel felt compelled to see the Essene commune, for in the ancient world people who left a corrupt society and went to live a life of purity and holiness, most of them unmarried, aroused in those who saw them a longing for purity in the dissolute world of those days. The Essenes were, therefore, famous throughout the world even before the discovery of the scrolls, but with the discovery we are able to learn the secrets of their interesting and surprising view of the world.

II.

Pharisees, Sadducees and Essenes

The Talmudic literature states that there were 24 sects in Israel, and at first glance this seems strange: How is it possible that, within the spiritual revolution common to the whole of Jewish society at the time of the Second Temple, the period that gave so much to mankind, there should have been that large a number of groups which fought against each other? Indeed the outstanding historian of the period, the priest Josephus, wrote that there were only three groups: Pharisees, Sadducees and Essenes. Judaism today is the spiritual heir of the Talmudic Sages, and is thus derived from the Pharisees.

How can one reconcile this three-fold division with the fact that there were so many sects? If we examine more closely the plentiful information we have in the apocryphal literature, in Josephus, in the scrolls and in the vast literature of the Talmudic Sages, we will see that the different small groups were related in some way, or were off-shoots of those three basic groupings in Judaism.

The great controversies in the world of the Sages, such as the one between the School of Hillel and that of Shammai, are well-known, but one cannot say that the School of Hillel and the School of Shammai, or the *hasidim* among them, were completely different groups. They all belonged to the group of Pharisee Sages.

With regard to the Sadducees, we know of the Sadducees themselves and of the Boethusians, who in fact shared the same outlook. It was one group with internal disagreements. Among the

Essenes there was a group which was somewhat different as regards organization and, apparently, also in outlook. It settled in Damascus, far from the borders of Eretz Israel, but nevertheless its document, the *Damascus Rule*, was found among the scrolls from the Dead Sea. In addition there was the group represented by John the Baptist, known from both Josephus and the New Testament. The outlook of John the Baptist can be examined in the light of the newly-discovered scrolls, to see how close he was to the Essenes. One can even conjecture that he had once been a member of their group. One should also mention the Zealots, the activist group which arose in the world of the Sages. The Zealots belonged to the Pharisee group. The three-fold division that Josephus established was, therefore, something he was aware of in reality, not merely an invention for the convenience of the Greek reader, who was, so to speak, searching for a parallel among the Jews to the philosophical schools with which he was familiar in his own world.

This division is hinted at in a way in a prayer which many of us say three times a day, that is the Eighteen Benedictions, also known as the *Amidah*.[4] After the benediction for the gathering-in of the exiles, which ends with the words: "Who gathers the banished ones of his people Israel," come three additional benedictions: "Restore our judges as of old," which in the shortened form of the *Amidah* known as *Havinenu*, is summarized by the words: "Those who have strayed from Your way will judge according to Your opinion." One cannot avoid the conclusion that, when this benediction was composed in antiquity, it was intended for one whose *halakhah* was misguided, and the hope was that those who taught a *halakhah* that was not in the way of God would repent and judge according to the correct *halakhah*. One can imagine that this is a reference to the Sadducees.

Many people consider the next benediction, the one concerning heretics, as having been intended against the Christians. But this is not the opinion of Jewish scholars today. This benediction, which refers to those who break away from the Jewish community, was apparently directed against the Essenes as well. The Essenes said of themselves, that they had turned away from walking in the ways of the people, relying on *Isaiah* 8:11 as they understood it. They saw in their separatism something desirable; they saw themselves as the "true Israel." It is clear that the unity of the nation could not tolerate this, and in this benediction we have an expression of a criticism of them which also included other groups.

In the third benediction, which opens with the words, "Toward the righteous," it is easy to identify the people who were the subject of the benediction: the community of Pharisee Sages, for it mentions "the righteous and the pious, the elders of thy people of the House of Israel, and the remnant of their Scribes." These are almost archaic terms, which have about them an echo of the Hasmonean period. So, we have three benedictions: one relating to criticism of the Sadducees and expressing the hope that they will mend their ways; the second referring to all those who believe it right to leave the way of the people, including among them the Essenes; and the third a reference to our community, the community of those who pray, the community of the Pharisees, the Sages.

If we remove these three benedictions from the framework of the *Amidah*, we will see that the benediction that precedes them speaks of God as the One who "gathers the banished of His people Israel," and the benediction that follows them ends with the words "who rebuilds Jerusalem"; we have here the two hopes for the End of Days, that of the ingathering of the exiles and that of the rebuilding of Jerusalem in the time to come. By removing the three benedictions hinting at the three groups we mentioned, one gets a saying parallel to a verse in the Psalms: "The Lord builds up Jerusalem: he gathers together the banished of Israel" (Psalm 147:2), but in the reverse order. This fact proves, in my view, that the three benedictions referring to the three groups were introduced into the prayer at a later stage. It is likely, as we can gather from the *Havinenu* version, that this was done at a time before all hope was lost for the repentance of the Sadducees. The three benedictions were all introduced roughly in the Hasmonean period, at the time of John Hyrcanus or Aristobulus, or at the beginning of the reign of Alexander Jannaeus.

17

It follows that not only Josephus, but also our prayer, divides the community of Israel into three groups. That is to say, this was not an artificial division which existed only in the minds of the members of the Dead Sea Sect,[5] who were accustomed in their commentaries on the Prophets and the Psalms to interpret biblical verses in contemporary terms, and who saw the words written in the Holy Scriptures as allusions to what was happening to them in their own time. For this reason, they used to construct what scholars call "typological interpretations" — the deeds of the fathers being regarded as a sign for the sons, as the Talmudic saying goes - and saw the division into tribes and kingdoms in the Biblical period as alluding to the divisions which occurred in their own time. There is no doubt that they saw themselves as Judah, for the Kingdom of Judah was sanctified by the presence in it of Jerusalem, and the Pharisees they identified with Ephraim. And it is not difficult to assume that they identified the Sadducees with Manasseh. Again, the same division into three groups.

They even went further and interpreted the three cities in the Book of Nahum as allusions to the same three groups: No-Ammon represented the Pharisees, Nineveh the Sadducees, and Jerusalem, in the spiritual sense of the word, Jerusalem on High as it were, as the Essenes themselves. The conclusion that we must of necessity draw from this is not only that the threefold division derived from Josephus was a division which existed in reality, or at least in the consciousness of Israel at that period, but also that the threefold division brings us close to certainty that the Dead Sea Sect were the Essenes. They hoped that at some time the truth of Judah would be revealed, and that then those who had been led astray by the Oral Law of the Pharisees, who were the unlearned, simple people, would return to the Essene truth, a hope which was not realized.

The Sadducees — Manasseh — are described in the *Commentary on Nahum* as fighters, warriors upon whom catastrophe has already fallen (an allusion to the time of Pompey), while the hope is that tribulation will yet come upon Ephraim, the Pharisees, something which did not materialize.

There is another interesting difference in the nature of the three groups in the scrolls. While the Sadducees are not worthy of being considered as a community comparable to the Essenes, the Pharisees are described as a community in the full sense, albeit one with mistaken views.

The Essenes accuse Ephraim — the Pharisees — of having chosen to follow the easy path of too much moderation in its religious practices. There are both similarities and differences (according to the scrolls) on other points between the community of the Pharisees and that of the Essenes. Both the Pharisees and the Essenes regarded themselves as representing the people of Israel. This belief was the dialectic reason for the creation of these groups.

It is worth remembering that the Pharisees were a particular group *within* the congregation of Israel, while the Essenes were a separatist sect *outside* it. The Essenes thought that if they refused to "walk in the way of this people," they were fulfilling the will of God in their separation, while the Pharisees referred to themselves as the Sages of *Israel*.

Apart from the desire to consider themselves the sole representative of the House of Israel, there was another element in the dialectic process of the creation of groups within Israel: the different degree to which these groups accepted the laws of purification in everyday life. Unfortunately, our information on this subject, as regards *halakhah*, is still defective, but it is clear that the Pharisees, in the strict meaning of the word, were the people who "consumed their everyday food in ritual purity." That is to say, they imposed upon themselves a strict ritual purity in daily life. It is clear from the sources that the degree of ritual purity of the congregation of the "pious ones" (the *hasidim*) who joined the Hasmoneans at the beginning of the revolt was higher than that of the Pharisees, and from the scrolls it appears that the degree of ritual purity of the Essenes was higher still. Incidentally, Josephus also mentions the Essenes' purification rituals.

But it should be remembered that among the Pharisees the members of the congregation who "consumed their everyday food in ritual purity" were only the nucleus of the movement, while among the Essenes, although there were certainly those who did not reach the point of taking upon themselves the full complex of purification laws, the goal was for them also to become full members of the sect.

Thus the particular purification laws created groups of people who differed in this from each other. There were people who sympathized with the Essenes, but did not take on themselves the full rigor of the life of purity, which was apparently one of the reasons for the creation of the closed society and the isolation from others.

Josephus tells us that, as regards ritual purity, there were at the time of Herod about 6,000 members of the Pharisaic congregation, probably those who undertook to "consume their everyday food in ritual purity," while there were about 4,000 such Essenes. At first sight this is not a great difference as regards numbers, but in fact there was a real difference, for the Pharisaic Sages did not insist that everyone should be a full member of the congregation; this was an open society of a broad movement based on certain points of "national consensus," as one would say today, and so was able to win the support of the people. We learn from the works of Josephus that the whole nation followed the Pharisees, even if the number of full members was relatively limited, while the Essenes had the task of winning the people's support to the extent of turning them into full members of the sect. The Essenes called such people "volunteers" — today one might use the term "candidates for membership." They lived within the framework of the sect for a certain period — two or three years — and then were accepted as full members of the sect. The Essenes regarded the nation's following of the Pharisees with astonishment and loathing, and compared this following of Sages to the worship of Baal in the First Temple period: the people were being misled by the deceivers among the Pharisees, who were Ephraim. The Essenes hoped that at the End of Days, when their truth, the truth of Judah, would be revealed, those simple and naive people who were not members of the Pharisaic congregation, would join Judah — the Essenes.

The Essenes developed a very particular view of the world, concentrated and closed, and similar, if one may say so, to ultra-orthodox Marxism, the good side of which was an acuity of vision, and the bad side the distortion inherent in vision which is far too sharp. We are, then, faced with a separatist group, one of the groups in which the splendor of the Second Temple period was expressed, and opposed to it a group from which there arose the teachers of the nation, the Pharisee Sages, whom the people followed, and opposed to both of them the Sadducees, who did not succeed in becoming a group with a message that could inspire the people.

III.

The Date of the Sect of the Scrolls

For information on the history of the Essenes, we must rely on both Josephus and the scrolls which have been published so far. There also exists one particular historic document, as yet unpublished, which mentions peoples' names. In those scrolls that belong to the type known as "apocalyptic literature" (literature which prophesies the ultimate redemption) people are not mentioned by name. The characters in the holy drama and the sacred conflicts are represented only by epithets and not by names. We still do not know the name of the founder of the Essene sect. It is known that he built the city — that is, the sect — and that his epithet was the Teacher of Righteousness. The leader of the Pharisees is referred to as the "Scoffer." The word "Pharisees" does not appear at all, but only the epithets the "Scoffer," or the "Spouter of Lies." Among the Sadducees we have the "Wicked Priest" or the "Lion of Wrath," and the question must be asked whether the "Lion of Wrath" was in fact identical to the "Wicked Priest." I once tried to describe the history of the Essenes in an article,[6] and I came to certain conclusions on the basis of this chain of terms, expressions and epithets.

On the question of the date when the Essenes began to exist, there is an interesting controversy. Catholic scholars, and a few Protestant scholars as well, believe that the three groups — Pharisees, Sadducees and Essenes — were all created at the time of Jonathan, the brother of Judah the Maccabee. This approach dates them to about 140 B.C.E. I do not know the reason why certain scholars push the date of the Essenes so far back, to a period which seems to me too early, apart from one incidental reference in Josephus, who says, speaking of the days of Jonathan, the brother of Judah, that at about that time there were three groups: Pharisees, Sadducees and Essenes (*Antiquities* XIII:171). Perhaps one of the three groups arose at that time, but Josephus himself first mentions the Essenes at the time of Aristobulus I, the heir of John Hyrcanus. Yet he only mentions events connected with the history of the Pharisees and Sadducees in the days of John Hyrcanus. The first Essene to whom he refers is Judah the Essene, mentioned in connection with a tragic incident. It is this incident which enables us to understand more deeply the nature of the Essenes, and in this way Josephus confirms what is found in the scrolls.

Josephus writes of this incident, which happened in about 100 B.C.E. (that is about 40 years after the time of Jonathan). Aristobulus, who was suspicious and cruel, invited his brother, Antigonus, to visit him. The latter, on the advice of some wicked people, wore armor, and was killed on the way to his sick brother, although this was not Aristobulus' fault.

At this time there lived in Jerusalem an Essene whose name was Judah, perhaps the Teacher of Righteousness himself, who had the "gift of prophecy." (Josephus says that the Essenes had this gift — that they could foretell the future.) Judah the Essene prophesied that Antigonus would be killed beside Strato's Tower.

Judah the Essene was shocked, and thought that he was mistaken in this, the first prophecy of his life. After all, Strato's Tower (the future Caesarea) was far away, and if Antigonus was now coming to see the king, how could he be killed in Caesarea, when the king was in Jerusalem? When the murder took place, it transpired that it took place actually near a little turret named Strato's Tower in Jerusalem. This is the first appearance of an Essene in Josephus and, as I said, he lived in Jerusalem.

Josephus first tells this story in the *Jewish Wars* and repeats it in the *Jewish Antiquities*. There he says that Judah the Essene was with his pupils and taught them how to understand the words of the

Prophets. As I stated earlier, the possibility cannot be ruled out that this Judah was the Teacher of Righteousness, the founder of the Essene sect. In the *Commentary on Habakkuk* (7:2-5) it is said of the Teacher of Righteousness, that it was he "to whom God set understanding that he might interpret all the secrets of the words of His servants, the prophets."

In another place (*Jewish Wars* II:159), we read that the Essenes knew the future, "being versed from their early years in holy books, various forms of purifications and aphorisms of prophets." There is in this some confirmation of the fact that the Essenes had contemporary interpretations for the words of the Prophets. According to Josephus, the first Essene mentioned by him, Judah the Essene, was already occupied with this in about 100 B.C.E..

The fact that the Essenes prophesied the future by deducing it from their interpretation of the Prophets is something we had learned from Josephus. Now we can see this, if one can put it that way, in black and white in the writings called *pesharim* (commentaries), in which the Essenes read the words of the Prophets and interpreted them in a contemporary sense.

Another story about the Essenes and their ability to prophesy relates to the Herodian period. It tells (Antiquities 15:373-379) of Menahem the Essene, a man older than Herod, who once, upon seeing Herod as a child, hit him and said: "You will be king, and you rule the realm happily ... but you will forget pity and justice." This seemed most improbable because, as the Hasmoneans were in power, it was not possible to imagine that Herod could become king. Herod was indeed the son of an important man, but he was certainly not a king. Moreover, he was not exactly of the seed of Israel. When Herod later became king, he summoned Menahem the Essene and asked him: "Tell me, how many years will I reign?" Menachem did not wish to answer. "Ten years, twenty?" — "Yes" — "Thirty years?" — "Yes" — "How many more?" The Essene was silent. Thus a special relationship arose between King Herod and the Essenes. Josephus relates that it was for this reason that Herod spared the Essenes, treated them warmly and did not demand that they pledge their allegiance to him.

Further evidence against Josephus' claim of the Essenes originating in 140 B.C.E. may be seen in the fact that the scholars who investigated Qumran dated the beginnings of the Essene settlement roughly to the period of Aristobulus I, or John Hyrcanus. This contradicts the incidental information of Josephus that the Essenes existed at the time of Jonathan, and confirms their appearance in the time of the later Hasmonean rulers (the people whom the Essenes referred to in contempt and hostility as "the last priests of Jerusalem"). Moreover, the scholars claim that there is a break in the settlement at Qumran in the Herodian period, and they assume that the Essenes left Qumran after an earthquake, which occurred in the year 30 B.C.E., and returned there only around the time of the birth of Jesus. It is difficult to establish whether this is correct from the archaeological point of view. There is apparently some evidence to suggest that Essenes were living in Qumran in the time of the Herodian famine.

Apart from Qumran, Essene cells were also established in other places, since we know from both the scrolls and other sources that there was even an Essene settlement in Jerusalem. (There is the Essene Gate on Mt. Zion, which was excavated by archaeologists.) If we accept the view that the Essene sect began in about 100 B.C.E., there is no doubt that Judah the Essene still lived in Jerusalem, but it is impossible to know with certainty whether he was the Teacher of Righteousness. (In my opinion, it is very probable.) It is also impossible to know exactly when the Essenes decided to leave the towns, "the dwellings of men of evil," and to gather at Qumran, and around Ein Gedi; when the community at Damascus was founded; when the Essenes decided to be less strict; when Qumran was left as a sort of center to which they always escaped, although they could maintain their splendid isolation in the towns as well; or when the groups — those little cells within the towns, which did not have to keep so strictly the commandment of separation from people and of going to the desert — were founded.

With the help of Josephus and of the scrolls, we have spread before our eyes a complete, colorful and variegated picture of the history of this important sect. The first Essene, the prophet who interpreted the Prophets, Judah the Essene, lived in Jerusalem in the tragic period around 100 B.C.E., at the time of Aristobulus I. When he foretold the death of Antigonus he was still living in Jerusalem, but when the sect coalesced and the persecutions began, the people left Jerusalem and settled mainly near Ein Gedi, in Qumran, and began their feverish intellectual activity. They developed their ideas and came into conflict with the other movements, the Pharisees and Sadducees; and the Teacher of Righteousness, the founder of the sect, was persecuted by them both, as a result of his desire for confrontation and the knowledge that he held in his own hands the absolute truth and the correct understanding of the Torah of Israel.

The Essenes consolidated and took on the form of an organized community, with a system of communal ownership. They founded other groups inside towns, which formed a sort of cells of theirs. Because of the persecution and out of their feverish spiritual activity, they looked on their surroundings with a skeptical eye, and saw the cruel "King of Flesh and Blood," Alexander Jannaeus, killing their enemies, the Pharisees, who requested help from the Greek king, Demetrius. They witnessed all the troubles preceding the invasion of Pompey in 63 B.C.E., and even before then, in the victory of the Sadducees in the period of Alexander. The victory of the Pharisees over the Sadducees in the reign of Alexandra Salome struck them as a national catastrophe, as if power had shifted from one tormentor to another. The saw the ineffectual rule of the queen, who was in their eyes a wicked queen. After this they witnessed the period of the Roman invasion, and saw as vengeance, although it pained them, the conquest of Jerusalem by Pompey and all the cruel events of that time. Then came the period of Herod, in which they lived in some form of uneasy peace, while the superstitious Herod made concessions to the Essenes, who he believed were no danger to his rule. This situation lasted until the period of the Great War, in which at least some of the Essenes were swept up in the national enthusiasm, and one of the leaders of the revolt was an Essene who fell near Ascalon.

Afterwards, the Essenes disappear from view, and are known only through their writings. It can be hoped that we will learn more of that fascinating history when the rest of their documents are published. The scrolls enable us to see history from another angle; we know of the Essenes from the writings of ancient authors, and indirectly from some pseudepigrapha. and now we know Jewish history in its greatness and its suffering, in a very clear light, from the writings of the Essenes themselves, from those scrolls which give us the opportunity to see the glory and the misery of our people's history in the distant past.

IV.

The Daily Life of the Sect and its Organization

The Essenes were regarded in the ancient world as a phenomenon that embodied ideals common to both a certain part of Judaism and to a large part of the ancient world in general. According to the Roman author Pliny, they were seen as a group which had abandoned the vanities of this world, elevated itself above the material world, attained a mystical consciousness, and renounced the luxuries that were a plague in the ancient world. They shut themselves up among the date palms, held their property in common, and did not marry, keeping their distance from the basic evil of sexual activity. They lived in special sanctity, as it were, and at the same time were also happy. "A whole city of happy people beside the Dead Sea," wrote Dio Chrysostom, a member of the school of Cynics who scorned civilization.

Even Josephus (who eventually became a Pharisee) lived among them for some time and learned from them. This idealized picture is reminiscent of the attraction in our own day of the kibbutzim, which are considered ideal societies. The Essenes used to say about themselves that, because of their special way of life, a life of modesty and frugality, that they reached a very old age. (In fact, the skeletons that have been found do not confirm an exceptional age for the Essenes.) This was an idealized picture, derived from a longing for purity. Jews and non-Jews admired the Essenes, particularly their practice of holding property in common, for many thought that communal property had characterized humanity before it was corrupted.

Now one can know about them not only from the accounts of contemporary authors (Philo of Alexandria, who gives an idealized picture of them, and Josephus, who "bends" the truth a little); and one can compare this information with what is found in the literature of the Essenes themselves, as far as this has been published. The basic information is confirmed, but is given a slightly different tone; one of stubborn people who left the society, but not exactly out of a desire to be complete pacifists, as they were described. They were pacifists, certainly, but at the same time prepared themselves for a war of world destruction, that world-wide revolution in which they would be the nucleus and the elite of Israel. On the other hand, the writings confirm their remarkable social organization, the common property and communal life, in isolation from others, both in their settlement at Qumran and in those in the towns.

Not everyone could undertake the rigor in religious practice and in daily life that they imposed on themselves, and I have already mentioned that there was a more moderate group living in Damascus, whose members were more open toward the world. This group also had slaves; the Essenes in Eretz Israel, on the other hand, did not, perhaps out of democratic egalitarianism, but perhaps also because they did not want to have Gentiles among them (Hebrew slaves hardly existed). Indeed, one of the most remarkable things revealed in the scrolls is the Essenes' hatred for Gentiles. The Essenes thought that the Gentiles were all condemned to destruction and could not be saved, a view which contradicted that of all the other Jewish groups and that of the Prophets as well.

If we could had visited Qumran, we would have seen how beautifully the town was built, the settlement isolated from the world, with a tower and bathing places in which they bathed daily, to maintain their ritual purity and to insist on their exclusivity.

One can guess that their community of property — which was a unique phenomenon at that time — arose for two reasons, the first being their high standards of purity. Their desire to live together required them to maintain a common standard of purity, and not to touch each other's money. (It is true that they had a treasury, but that was the property of the sect, the holy men.) Secondly — and this was the more basic reason — the community of property derived from the group's ideological unity. This society, which from a certain point of view appears an egalitarian one, was not at all egalitarian as regards spiritual and organizational ranking, but only as far as its community of property, which was part of the contempt in which its members held property altogether. "The last priests of Jerusalem," the last Hasmoneans, were accused by the Dead Sea Sect of accumulating the wealth of Gentiles. The Essenes themselves despised the Gentiles and their money, and saw these as something negative. Nevertheless, the group was fairly rich, for it collected its money in a common treasury. Thus, as Philo of Alexandria says, there were no rich and no poor. There existed the capital of the holy men, the size of which is not known.

The Essenes employed themselves growing dates, in producing "date honey" (it should not be assumed that they kept bees, as the sources say), and at working in the fields, and saw this as their way of life. There is a very important additional aspect to their community of property, in that they differentiated between their communal property and the property of others. In negotiations with others they were certainly tougher than Shylock, and one can see this both from Josephus and from the scrolls.

They were forbidden to give gifts to their relatives without the permission of their leaders. Everyone who joined their society had to surrender all his property. They wished to renounce "the wealth of the men of evil." That is to say, they maintained a kind of separatism on the subject of wealth as well. They saw everyone else as the world of evil, and so they spoke of "the wealth of rape," "the wealth of the men of evil," with which they wanted no contact. There existed among them a combination of communism and hatred toward the rest of the world. They were thus very similar to the Christian groups that followed in their footsteps; groups which maintained community of property and separatism from the world, which was supposed to hate them. They saw themselves, like the

Essenes, as groups of the enlightened, destined to conquer the other, wicked world. This picture of the Essenes, as it is painted, is not a pleasant and ideal one.

Josephus stresses that they did not marry, but examination of the skeletons found in the excavations have revealed, without doubt, that there were women there. The Roman author Pliny also says that they did not have wives, but Josephus, who knew that some of them did, speaks of those who were married. That is to say, there were those who decided that, in order for the human race not to disappear from the world, it was worthwhile to marry. I assume that fairly many did have wives, but here we should note an important phenomenon: the Essenes who did marry accepted marriage to one woman only, that is monogamy. In fact, at that time most Jews were monogamous. It is not known, for example, that any of the Sages had more than one wife, although they were permitted to do so. In contrast, for the Essenes, this was a law. They maintained that as entry into the Ark was two by two, and as Adam and Eve became one flesh from two, it meant that the reproductive unit was monogamy. But since those who married did so only in order to "be fruitful and multiply," there was an engagement period, and only when the woman became pregnant did they marry. The origin of this custom was that among them, as in Christianity later on (and this was inherited from the Essenes), there was no possibility of divorce. In order for the marriage to be valid, an Essene man could marry only after the age of twenty, "when he knew what to do." That is more or less what is written in the scrolls. We do not know of sex education among them, but in this way they ensured monogamy and the prevention of divorce.

There are scholars who consider the possibility that the women's skeletons were those of celibate Essene women, that is of women who decided not to marry and came there to live in complete chastity, like Christian nuns, but one should not assume that all Essenes were celibate.

Josephus and the philosopher Philo of Alexandria, say that they did not marry because in a communal society like this women only cause confusion and dispute, but I imagine that the reason was an increasing antipathy to sexual activity. They thought that the flesh was a kind of contamination, and that it was possible to attain a higher degree of purity if they refrained from marriage. I assume that this tendency grew among them, and that in the first century it was, perhaps, the governing view, but there was no rule forbidding marriage.

As regards the organization of the society, we have already mentioned that the Essenes lived under economic communism, and isolated themselves from the "men of evil." Over the communal property, they appointed men known as "inspectors" or "supervisors." These people had the authority to give gifts to the poor, or to receive guests. There is a certain paradox here: they regarded those around them with hostility, yet received unlimited visitors.

The inspector, or the supervisor, was also in charge of accepting new members, and of classifying the members according to rank. Everyone had his fixed place to sit and, once a year, apparently at the Feast of Shavuot, they swore the oath of allegiance to their covenant; each man's place was then assigned according to his ranking in faith and works. It was, therefore, both an egalitarian society and a hierarchic one. The Essenes' places were decided not only according to their different ranks (Josephus speaks of four ranks), but even when they held a general meeting of the cell, or of the community of Qumran, they sat in their regular places. It all becomes even more complicated because there was also a great difference among them between the priests and the ordinary people. (We do not know much about their attitude to Levites.)

The most important people among them were priests of the House of Zadok. In Jewish society at that time, the priesthood was also important in the leadership. Most of the important people of whom we know, including Josephus, were priests. Thus, there were differences between people even within the established hierarchic society, despite their communal property and common ideology.

The supervisor, who was also in charge of accepting new members, held a great deal of power in his hands. Josephus says (though this has not yet been found in the scrolls) that while everything else in Essene society was determined according to people's status, only the officials — the supervisors — were elected by everyone together. Election by the local Essenes decided who would be the officials. It seems to me that the election of the supervisors by the community of the members offered the possibility of correction, for it was the supervisor who controlled the community's property and made decisions about the acceptance of new members and the ranking of every member of the community. Thus the election of the supervisors by all members served as a correction to the hierarchical order of the sect.

The Dead Sea Sect, the Essenes (now one can say this with certainty) held general meetings, which lasted a long time. On the one hand they had to guard the secrets of their faith from outsiders; on the other it was possible to speak openly at this meeting. It was forbidden to be silent, from fear of the "spirit of apostasy," as they called it in their language, and thus they could introduce innovations into their ideology. Their communal meals were famous: the priests prepared the food, so that it should be ritually pure, and it was they who pronounced the first benedictions. They ate simple food with only one course and bread, and there was complete silence. The Essene meal had the atmosphere of a temple.

Thus, there was a common meal, communal life, and a society which closed itself to outsiders. Their particular social framework not only expressed their isolationism, but also gave them their communal life, their *yahad* (community), which made possible their feverish activity of spiritual creativity and their defined view of the world. This small society of Essenes, numbering a few thousand people, left its traces on the history of humanity as a whole, down to the present day.

V.

The Sect and the Rest of Israel

We have before us a closed sect with a very particular and well-established way of thinking, which did not identify with the rest of the nation. Its problem was how it could represent the whole nation, as the "true Israel." So it referred to itself as "Israel walking in the way of perfection," regarded itself as the elect, and thought that every non-sectarian Jew was not completely "Israelite," and in some respects stood on a level with the Gentiles: both the rest of Israel and the Gentiles were, in the group's eyes, vanity. It saw itself (as the Church later saw itself) as the only true religion in the world, and the rest of the world, which did not accept its faith, its teachings and its way of life, was doomed to perdition.

This extreme position, which almost has no parallel in modern separatist sects, was characteristic of the Dead Sea Sect, and brought it into conflict with the two great schools in Judaism, both with the Pharisees, who entered into violent disputes with it, and with the Sadducees, who persecuted it. This determined the Essenes' position in the world, and their future influence, in particular on Christianity. They are an example of a kind of people who, although they knew what they wanted, began to have doubts, and made problems for themselves. In other words, this was a sect which thought that it alone had received a unique revelation of God. Selection and isolationism had, in the Essenes' opinion, existed since the beginning of Israel's history. Just as the Ten Tribes had been lost and Judah, Benjamin and half of the tribe of Levi had survived, so the Essenes themselves were the real Israel, different from the rest of the nation, to whom God, through the Prophets and through the founder of the sect, had revealed the truth.

An interesting dialectical situation was created here. On the one hand, the Essenes thought they had to isolate themselves from others because they were the true Israel, and they sentenced the rest of Israel to damnation; but on the other hand they were interested in attracting as many people as possible, so that they should accept their ideas, join the sect and live with them their peculiar, isolated life, different from that of the rest of Israel, in both its ideological collectivism and its organization.

It is paradoxical that an isolationist sect, which hated others and isolated itself from them, earned many people's respect, because they regarded it and its members as idealists and perfect human beings. Thus, both Jews and Gentiles spoke of the Essenes with admiration. They were different from the Pharisees. The Pharisees — that is to say the Sages — also believed that they represented the true belief, the true attitude of the People of Israel. This belief, though, was not merely that of the full members of the Pharisee community, but also of those connected with it, who joined it as "pupils of the Sages," and were not required to become full members. As against the conception of the Essenes, who regarded themselves as the elite, or as the only Israel which existed, the Pharisees were interested in making as many disciples as possible.

There was, therefore, something revolutionary in the Essene world view. That can also be said for the ideal of poverty, expressed through community of property. Hence, among the Essenes, more than any other stream in Judaism, a socialist, revolutionary way of thought was emphasized. The Essene loathing of wealth was connected with the idea of opposition to the rich. As they understood it, wealth — private wealth, of course — interfered with one's being the elect of God.

The Essenes associated the idea that they were the chosen ones of righteousness, the elect of God, as they called it, with the socialist idea. Although they despised the Gentiles, they claimed that the last Hasmonean priests were wicked because they had accumulated wealth, and not only the wealth of Israel, but also that of the Gentiles. In other words, the Essenes had an anti-imperialist attitude, although they did not accept the idea of universalism. as do modern anti-imperialist theories. They came to the conclusion that it was wrong to exploit even those Gentiles who were doomed to destruction, because all amassing of wealth, all external political power, was to them something contemptible.

Their socialism, almost revolutionary communism, was unique among the Jews of the period. The attitude of the Sages was that the poor must be cared for, loved, helped; that destitution was a situation that required correction, while the Essenes saw poverty as a religious attainment.

There was an internal tension between the idea of their being the elect and the idea of revolution. If someone sees himself as being a chosen individual, it can be assumed that he will not be very sensitive to the problems of the external world. The Essenes found particular solutions to these problems from their own narrow point of view, and so their revolutionary ideas were expressed through denying the existence of things of all kinds: world order, the beliefs of the rest of the nation, and even the rejection of the Temple of their time, and the hope of an ideal Temple as they wished to see it. For this reason they moved away from the worship in the Temple and did not sacrifice in it. They valued Jerusalem as the city of the Temple, but could not participate in worship in the Temple, because in their opinion it had not been built correctly. They rejected both the priesthood and the existing *halakhah*, and regarded the *halakhah* and the opinions of the rest of Israel as being clearly separatist and sectarian. Their main point of departure was the existing Jewish *halakhah*, but they changed part of this in a sectarian, rigoristic manner.

A verse in *Isaiah* (8:11) states: "... He turned me from walking in the way of this people."[7] As the Essenes saw it, the fact that they turned from walking in the way of the people was positive. They were the elect of God; they were the true Israel; they were the ones who lived by the right calendar, which was different from that used by the rest of Israel. They were, therefore, the ones who did right in the world, for they obeyed the message of the Torah of Israel in its fullest sense, while neither the Pharisees nor the Sadducees could equal them in strictness. They claimed that on questions of *halakhah* the Pharisees chose the easy way. So the Essenes had not only a special sectarian *halakhah*, different from the daily living habits of the rest of the nation, but also a conservative *halakhah*. We learn from the sources of the strictness of the Sabbath regulations which they obeyed in every detail. Some people even thought that on Sabbaths they even refrained from performing their natural functions, so that they should not have to go outside (Josephus, *Jewish War* II:147). Josephus also states that when one saw a group of Essenes walking, they looked like school children afraid of their teacher (*Jewish War* II:126). They could apparently be recognized (like extreme Christian sects later) by their downcast eyes, their peculiar behavior and their white clothes.

In any case, this sect isolated itself and developed its own revolutionary ideas, which were expressed not only in the rejection of what existed in the world, but in fact in the desire to destroy it. Thus these people, who were believed to be pacifists and who refused to serve in the army, actually intended not only to conquer the whole of Eretz Israel and to change all the incorrect practices in the Temple, but even to conquer the entire world. From their point of view, therefore, there was no contradiction between their extreme separatism, dictated by the idea of being the true Israel, and their warlike ideas expressed, among other places, in the *Scroll of the War of the Sons of Light against the Sons of Darkness*. This describes a war according to God's will, a Utopian war, in which they would first conquer Eretz Israel and in later years the rest of the world.

A certain tension is created here, and we will return to this point when we discuss their view of the world, expressing their attitude toward it, an attitude which was both practical and impractical at the same time. It was clear to them that they had to keep away from politics and to treat each other well, but they also had to hate the rest of the world. It was their duty to hate all the "Sons of Darkness," for they themselves were the only "Sons of Light." They had to hate the world and the rest of Israel in secret, that is not to reveal their hatred, but to develop their secret doctrines, which they were forbidden to reveal to others, and to develop their secret hatred of the rest of the world. Even if externally they appeared very pleasant in the way they received their guests, we now know from the scrolls their hidden attitude, which they certainly did not disclose in public. It was a doctrine of hatred toward the world outside and toward the rest of the Jews, who were condemned to a terrible punishment which would overtake them. One can imagine their saying to their guests, "How nice to see you. Come in and sit down. Stay with us." And we can almost hear the Essene's internal voice saying, "I have deceived him with love. Now I was kind to him, I treated him with love; and I reserve my right to do so. God will punish him in the course of time, but no one can tell when this will happen. Meanwhile, I must behave toward the world, toward the rest of Israel, as a slave toward his master, must leave him all his wealth and everything he has, and not hasten the time of the revolution. I must behave to him out of what can be called 'conditional pacifism' and must make concessions to the rest of the world, so that, when the time comes, God will wreak His vengeance upon it."

The Essenes were, so to speak, activists who paralysed themselves by self-restraint and by their hopes for the future, because they could not know when the Day of Judgment would come. It was precisely the Utopian basis of their separatism which enabled them to say that while they were the poor now and had turned from walking in the way of the people, in the future they would be the princes and the leaders. This, then, led to their developing this friendly attitude toward others, which was in some respects a false friendliness. There are examples of similar occurrences in modern history as well.

The Essenes were waiting for the Judgment Day, but the Judgment Day did not come. Herod knew that they were not dangerous. He preferred them to others, apparently because he saw the Utopian, unrealistic element in their hatred, and knew that they would do nothing against him.

It must not be forgotten that there was an additional tension in their approach. Apart from the tension between hatred and love, there was also a tension between their separatism and their desire to rule. As there was a desire to rule, it meant there was also a desire to win over the rest of Israel — as followers. The group's separatism was, therefore, connected, in a dialectical way, with the idea of mission and saving souls. How far it succeeded in this, and whether the outside world realized the group's hatred toward it, or only saw what was apparent, is impossible to say.

When I read Josephus, I have the impression that he knew these things, but did not disclose them in public. If this was indeed the group's view, we have here one of the most interesting and unusual phenomena in the history of mankind: on the one hand, it was a group which regarded itself as the "true Israel" and which stressed renunciation and isolationism, while on the other, it desired to conquer Israel. Here there were ideas of isolationism and community of wealth coupled with observation and interest in what was happening in the world, in order to know when the Judgment Day would come. Seclusion — and social awareness.

VI.

The House of Israel and the Sect

The Dead Sea Sect is apparently identical with the Essene sect which we already know. We know of the Essenes, the Pharisees and the Sadducees from the period of John Hyrcanus onwards or, more precisely, we hear of the Essenes from the time of his successor. One may therefore ask whether the Essenes arose after the Hasmonean wars, or whether some quasi-Essenes existed even before this period. Establishing this point will greatly affect our understanding of the group. Those who assume that the Essenes existed even before the Hasmonean wars must assume that they, or their forerunners, took part in those wars. And in fact some people do identify them with the *hasidim* (pious ones) who joined Mattathias, the son of John and father of Judah the Maccabee.

Although this conjecture that identifies the Essenes with the *hasid* community is extremely ancient, already appearing in the tenth century in the book of *Josippon*, it has no basis in fact. It seems to me more helpful to see the origins of the Essenes in a sect which was formed in the later Hasmonean period (what the Essenes referred to as the time of "the last priests of Jerusalem"), and to see it, at least from the historical point of view, as a consequence of the disappointment felt by certain people in Jerusalem over the failure to maintain the purity of morals and decent standards of combat practiced by the first Hasmoneans.

The Essenes should not, therefore, be identified with the *hasidim*. Moreover, not only did they never call themselves *hasidim*, but the

40

word does not even appear in their sectarian writings.[8] Nor does the word *ge'ulah* (redemption), or its root *g'al* appear (except in quotations from the Bible). They apparently disapproved of that secular redemption of which the Hasmoneans prided themselves and which later served as a slogan for others who fought against Rome. They rejected the purely political aspect of this redemption to such a degree that they even avoided the use of the root *g'al* in the sense of *ge'ulah* (redemption) and used it only in the word *megu'alim* (unclean). They even used to link verses in such a way that the use of the word would be avoided.[9]

This movement, founded by the Teacher of Righteousness, was a response of those disappointed in the situation, who for this reason created an isolationist sect with disillusionment as one of its leading sentiments.

A sect like this could not in any way come to terms with the other movements. The Teacher of Righteousness, who apparently lived more or less in the period of Alexander Jannaeus, was persecuted by the other two movements in Judaism. According to the scrolls, he was persecuted both by the Pharisees (the Sages, those called "seekers of falsehood," that is people whose doctrine was a doctrine of falsity) and by the Sadducees, who had the power. Members of the sect refer with hatred to Alexander Jannaeus, and with equal loathing to the leader of the Pharisees, whom they call "the Scoffer" and "the Spouter of Lies."

We do not know the name of the founder of the sect, only his epithet, the Teacher of Righteousness. He founded the sect as a separate community, a kind of "holy city," a heavenly Jerusalem, as opposed to the Pharisee community. It can be assumed that at first the Teacher of Righteousness appealed to the Pharisee leader, hoping to persuade him of the truth of his teachings. It is likely that he also sent him a letter explaining his position, and of course expected a negative response. But what he evidently did not expect was persecution, not only by the priests of Jerusalem, the Sadducees, by the later Hasmoneans, but also by the Pharisees. The Sadducees were a group of rich and powerful men, brave and strong, the priests and commanders of the Hasmonean army, an army of

41

mercenaries. While the Sadducees had a superficial philosophy, the Sages developed a complete system of doctrines with an open view of the world. But before the Roman period they too were ready to persecute others. From the works of Josephus, we can learn how in the reign of Queen Salome Alexandra the Pharisees persecuted the Sadducees and killed some of them. Echoes of religious persecution are to be found in the *Scroll of Hymns*, which in my opinion belongs to a fairly late stage of the sect. There the Pharisees come to the author of the *Hymns* (who was an important figure in the sect at that time), and try to persuade him (and even threaten his life and that of the sect) to accept the Pharisee doctrine, to turn from the real truth of the sect to the truth of the "seekers of falsehood."[10]

The Pharisees were also persecuted at that time. I imagine that the persecutions by the Pharisees ended more or less at the time when the Romans gained control of the country, after Herod, or even during his reign, when the Pharisees, according to many sources, had already become more moderate. The Essenes too, the Dead Sea Sect, became more mystical, once they conceived their doctrine as more spiritual, as withdrawal from the flesh. In this period they apparently became more moderate (it is not known whether they also became more open), and presented no particular threat to the world of the Sages, although some protests against the Pharisees were still heard from the Essene side. As a result of their turning to mysticism and their withdrawal from the world, the Essenes began to be seen as perfect saints, living in the desert or in small groups in cities, and living at the highest pitch of holiness. A description of this kind is found in Josephus, who evidently knew of their hatred, but could still present them as perfect saints.

Apparently, a change took place among the Essenes. The ideology of hatred certainly remained, but the Essenes became more mystical, the Pharisees stopped persecuting their enemies (including the Sadducees), and the nation accepted the Pharisees' views. Then a process began in which the Essenes not only isolated themselves, but were also isolated by others. They were considered a sect of saints, who could no longer do harm to others. So Josephus could describe them positively. In the war against the Romans, there were some Essenes who joined the great revolt. We know of John the Essene who was an officer in the rebel army and fell in battle. At first sight this was a sort of "happy ending," in which the Essenes found their place among the nation, but in fact it was a very, very sad ending in which the Essenes disappeared.

Herod can serve as an instructive example. In his cunning he knew how to come to terms with all streams in Judaism. He understood that the Essenes were less dangerous than certain groups among the Sages. He reasoned that, despite their underlying hatred, that hatred would not be expressed, so he treated them with tolerance and allowed them to live their own lives. This is a common process in the history of sects: a distinct sect emerges; at first everyone hates it; then it appears that it is possible to live with it. But there were, of course, great differences between the world of the Sages and that of the Essenes, and between them both and the Sadducees, not only in matters of religious belief, but also in matters of religious practice. If Josephus had joined the Essenes he would have cut himself off from the rest of the nation, he would have deprived himself of any possibility of advancement, and we would not have had Josephus.

The use of their own calendar was the most particular way in which members of the sect differentiated themselves from the rest of Israel. They celebrated their festivals on different dates, with the deliberate intention of differentiating themselves from the other Jews. This is a phenomenon typical of many sects throughout the world. Even among the Jews, the Samaritan calendar is different from the Karaite one, and both differ from the common Jewish one. The calendar of the Sages, of the whole House of Israel, was different from the Essene one not only in the dating of the festivals, but in its whole conception of the year. The Essenes had a sophisticated solar calendar, in which there were fifty two weeks, and the festivals always began on the same day of the week. In this they were different from other Jews, who lived by a lunar calendar. What is not yet known from the writings already published, or from those apocryphal works close to the Essenes and using the same calendar, is whether they had intercalation, without which their calendar would not even fit the solar year. They succeeded in living according to this calendar of their own, on which they did much research, and which we also now know from the *Temple Scroll*. Moreover, they also had additional festivals, not recognized by other Jews, and a different *halakhah*. It was, therefore, inevitable that they came into conflict with the Sages, who wanted to impose their own *halakhah* on the whole House of Israel.

We know of a Sadducee priest who attacked the Teacher of Righteousness and his group on the sect's *Yom Kippur*, which was not the *Yom Kippur* recognized by other Jews.[11] Even so holy a day, one respected even by non-religious Jews, was held on a different date.

Here a very strange thing should be mentioned. The Essenes had a *halakhah*, but they had no concept of the Oral Torah. They did everything according to revelation. Sometimes one gets the impression that they in fact accepted the *halakhah* of the House of Israel and adapted it to their own tastes, without acknowledging the fact. They apparently saw this as a private revelation, although their conclusions were similar to those of the Oral Torah. For example, they had the custom of *eruv*, but they did not explain that it was a *halakhah* of the Oral Torah, but established it as their own rule, although the two were identical, or at least similar. They saw the origins of the sect's *halakhah* in an interpretation of the Torah, or as a private revelation to the sect's members. They had not only a special *halakhah* destined for the sect, which they did not expect outsiders to practice and did not believe was required of them, but also a *halakhah* for the whole House of Israel. They wished to impose their particular practices on the rest of Israel, but the rest of Israel refused to accept them. In this way the breach between them and the Sages grew wider. The Sages saw them as a disruptive element which destroyed the unity of the people in the area of everyday practice as well as of doctrine, and could not accept a group which refused to acknowledge their supremacy.

The situation was such that the Essenes said that the Sages "withhold from the thirsty the drink of knowledge, and assuage their thirst with vinegar" (*Hymns* IV:11). That is to say, the Sages did not teach the people true doctrine, but prevented them from accepting the Essene truth, and gave them vinegar instead of wine.

There was also an essential difference between the Sages and the Essenes in regard to Oral Torah: the Essenes had no concept of an Oral Torah passed down from one teacher to another. It was their custom to write down their teachings. In contrast, from a certain date it was usual for the Sages not to record the Oral Torah, so that it would be a living current. This led to the distinction between the House of Israel, which followed the Sages and was prepared to learn and preserve the Oral Torah, and the Essenes, whose writings were ever increasing.

VII.

The Doctrine of Predestination

The Dead Sea Sect was a unique phenomenon in its separatism, its isolation from the world, and its philosophical, theological and religious spirit. It was the only group within Second Temple Judaism to develop a systematic theology. It was one of the great virtues of the Sages' system to leave things open and to establish only basic guidelines to their approach. In contrast, the Dead Sea Sect, in the paradoxical restriction of its ideas, created a system which later influenced the history of all mankind. Its concentration, its logical and unrealistic way of thought, its extreme conclusions which did not correspond with reality, introduced into the entire world ideas over which men have debated and agonized every since.

The views of the Dead Sea Sect and the way it saw the world order were connected, as another side of the same coin, with its isolationism and its centralized organization. The Essenes were, so to speak, elevated above the world, in fact not of this world at all, but nevertheless living within it. They believed that they lived in the company of the angels; they were the "Congregation of God" (what the Christians later called the "City of God"), and they actually used images of a spiritual Temple City, differentiated in this from the others. They were the elect of God.

The great basic idea, which the Teacher of Righteousness apparently gave the world and which differed from those of similar movements of his age, was the doctrine we call the doctrine of predestination. Its basic idea was that everything was predetermined by God and could not be changed. That this was the Essenes' doctrine is stated explicitly, in black and white, by Josephus.[12] The doctrine of extreme predestination by God is found in the scrolls, just as Josephus states it was Essene doctrine. This identity of teachings is one of the strongest proofs that the Essenes and the Dead Sea Sect were one and the same.

One scholar who lived before the discovery of the scrolls correctly understood the social significance of this doctrine for the.Essenes. He stated that the doctrine of predestination was certainly what enabled the Essenes to see themselves as the elect of God.[13] In other words, if one sees oneself as exclusively chosen by God, or the sect as the City of God, as the true Israel, then this was ordained by God before the creation of the world. Even in modern Christian sects, following Calvin, the doctrine of predestination serves as a foundation for the ideology of the "City of God." Their adherents are the elect, they are the holy warriors, they are the ones who were predestined by God in an exclusive ordinance, "the Elect of His Will" in the language of the sect. But these are only the social implications. We must also understand that the doctrine of predestination, according to which everything is predetermined by God, is also a logical, though unrealistic, conclusion of the idea of the one God as the Prime Cause.

It is worth expanding on this point, which is usually misunderstood. When I say that tomorrow will be hot, I am deducing this from signs that foretell what is likely to happen. But if God knows that on a certain day it will be hot, or that someone will be killed or be born, then His knowledge is also what He has preordained. According to human logic, God knows everything in advance. I can know in advance, if I see certain signs, that a certain couple are going to get divorced. But my knowledge will not determine what is going to happen. Determining the facts is not under my control, while God's pre-knowledge is also predetermination.

The Essenes, whose approach may have originated in social reasons, were more consistent than those who say: "All is in the hand of God, except the fear of God." In the Essenes' opinion, such a statement limits the omnipotence of God who, according to their logic, cannot surrender the fear of God to a human decision. The Pharisees believed in providence, not in predestination, so that they could argue that things might change. That is to say, they stated that God sees everything and decides everything, but man can change things in the sphere of good and evil. If a man repents, like the people of Nineveh in the *Book of Jonah* for example, God can change His mind and not punish them. In such cases, the Essenes would say that God could not change His mind, for the repentance of Nineveh was also predetermined. For this reason the term "repentance" acquired a different meaning among the Essenes from the one it had for other Jews. The elect Essene was a person whose election was predetermined. He lived within the world, and it was predetermined that at a certain date he would leave the vanities of the world, enter the sect and accept its discipline and rules, and live as one of the Sons of Light, of the true Israel. The Essenes called this turning point, ordained by God, "repentance," and the covenant of the sect was called the "Covenant of Repentance" (*Damascus Rule* XIX:16). Accordingly, they could say that whoever joined the sect was repenting and returning to the Torah of our Teacher, Moses. Their "repentance" was what we would call "conversion": a man changes his ways not only in the sense that so far he has been evil and now has become good, but he also attains salvation through an inner light, through having already been made of the elect ones and thus finding the place ordained for him.

There were three views on divine providence, three schools: the Pharisees, Sadducees and Essenes. The Pharisees believed in providence but left man a certain freedom, a kind of "cooperation" as the Sages saw it between man and God. The Sadducees did not believe in providence; according to them, free will was absolute; the Essenes stressed that there was not only providence, but even unalterable predestination. "From the God of knowledge is all the present and future, and before they came to be He prepared all their pattern; and when they come to be at the times decreed for them it is as the pattern of His glory that they will fulfill their actions, and they cannot be changed" (1Q53:15-16).

48

There is, nevertheless, also an additional element here: the Essenes (like the Protestants, who learned it from the New Testament) not only had the idea of predestination, but also the idea of dualism. The dualism of good and evil had already appeared in Jewish thought in the Bible, and among the Essenes it developed into the diametrical contrast between the Sons of Light and the Sons of Darkness. God not only preordained what would happen, but He had also preordained the division into two rival camps confronting one another: from the source of light came all the generations of the Sons of Light, and from the source of darkness came all the generations of the Sons of Darkness. Perhaps there is some Persian influence here, since the Persians also had a dualistic doctrine of light and darkness, but the Persians did not associate this with the final destiny of the two camps, determinism according to which everything is preordained and cannot be changed.

One of the basic components of Essene predestination was the dualistic division into two camps, the righteous and the wicked. This belief caused many problems, which can be seen in the scrolls. If someone was predestined before the creation of the world to be a son of Light and then became a Son of Light, returned to the Torah of Moses and joined the sect, then, according to this belief, he should be preserved by God Himself from suffering and from sin. But this approach was not realistic, and so another element was added: that this division into good and evil also exists in the world of spirits. There were under God not only two camps of men, but also two camps of spirits, of angels. The subject of angels was very sacred, and it was forbidden to reveal the names of angels to outsiders (Josephus, *Jewish War* II:141). We have in the scrolls lists of angels written in code, although these have not yet been published.

There are two camps of spirits, the spirits of deceit and the spirits of truth. At the head of the spirits of deceit stands Belial, the sect's Satan, and opposing him stands the archangel Michael; God has ordained that everything that happens in the world is done through these two; two camps which will fight in the wars of the Sons of Light and the Sons of Darkness. An ordinary person, even one who

49

believed in predestination, would say that if someone caught a cold, it happened because he had sinned, or because he had been chilled. In the Essene way of looking at it, if one of the righteous ones caught a cold, it resulted from the activity of Belial, since God allowed him to hurt the righteous as well as the wicked. Moreover, while this righteous person was apparently one of the Sons of Light and ought not to sin, there is no one who does not sin a little. The Essenes' explanation for this was that the sins of the righteous come about through the activities of the forces of evil, for God grants to the spirits of deceit, to Belial, the possibility that the righteous should sin a little.[14]

We can see from this how far even such a solid and perfect system, when subjected to the test of reality, had to adapt its arguments and change course, just like astronauts who have to change the direction of their spaceship when it has deviated from its route because of some fault.

We have seen that the Sons of Light suffer and sin because God allows Satan and his followers to tempt them, to confuse them and to cause them suffering. But the members of the sect were so egocentric and so closed in on themselves that, in the scrolls so far published, there is not the slightest explanation of the question whence the Sons of Darkness derived their ascendancy and their prosperity. Some have claimed that the belief that everything is predestined leads people to inactivity, to fatalism, but there is a great deal of difference between fatalism and belief in a dualistic predestination which differentiates between the just and the unjust. The person who believes that he is the elect of God according to God's ordinance will wish to prove himself, to prove that he is not one of the Sons of Darkness. This desire leads him to feverish activity, and he lives with the terrible fear lest it should emerge that he has insinuated himself unworthily into this company of saints, and that he is doomed to hell. One of the nice points about this and very instructive of human nature, is that it is very hard to imagine that any of the sect would reach the conclusion that he was among the damned and begin to behave completely wickedly. Everyone wished to be "top of the class." The success of groups like these, which encourage a person to strenuous efforts to prove to himself and to others that he is among the Sons of Light, is based on these premises. Among the Essenes it reached the point where those who were punished and expelled from the sect because of some offence committed under the influence of Belial would not decide that they were condemned to hell, but would argue that the offence was only the result of a temporary error under the influence of the forces of evil. This is the reason why those expelled from the sect, as Josephus says (*Jewish War* II:143-144), continued to obey the purity laws and could not eat with the "Sons of Deception," who were condemned as transgressors and sinners. These outcasts thus almost starved to death, unless the sect eventually took pity on those it had expelled and allowed them to return. Such was the extent to which the idea of dual predestination influenced the sect, and it was one of the secrets of its success.

VIII.

The Conflict between Spirit and Flesh

We have stressed one point of importance for understanding the Essenes: their dualistic belief in predestination, which is important for the whole course of human history. This belief was derived from their view of God as omnipotent and all-governing: that if He knew in advance what was going to happen, that meant that He had also preordained it. This belief was linked with another ideology, connected with their idea of themselves as the exclusive elect of God: the dualistic belief that saw the world as divided into the Sons of Light and the Sons of Darkness. The Sons of Light were mainly the elect of the sect, those chosen by God according to His own decision before the creation of the world. All the rest, the other Jews and the Gentiles, were condemned to hell. The Essenes therefore developed their love for the Sons of Light and their hatred for the Sons of Darkness, since God created His world on the basis of this dualism.[15] This was the dualism of two opposing camps, one of which, that of the wicked, would eventually be destroyed. That is, eventually "all wickedness will go up as smoke," as is said in the *Rosh Hashanah* prayers. Wickedness would disappear in the War of the End of Days, and then the wicked would be defeated and only the righteous would remain.

The Essenes associated the idea of the division of humanity into two rival camps with the idea of predestination. An interesting development, of basic importance, took place within the Dead Sea Sect. At first the members had the idea of two opposing camps, facing each other with a clear-cut division between them. But in a later development the Dead Sea Sect arrived at an additional scheme, another dualism, which did not contradict the first one.

A person belonging to the elect was chosen by the decision of God before the creation of the world to be good or evil, and nothing could alter that. The righteous belonged to the sect by the choice of God. In the sect there arose the view that people are basically evil. The evil inclination works within a person and the impure element is present within him from birth to old age.[16] Man stands, as the sect's members put it, "in the sphere of sinful guilt." This feeling of loathing for basic humanity grew among the sect in the course of time. This element was not unknown in the ancient world, even outside the Essenes, and hints of it can be seen in Greek philosophy. At a later stage of their development, the Essenes called the evil element "flesh," and it was the corporeal element which led a person into the realm of impurity, not only ritual impurity from which an Essene could cleanse himself by purification and repentance, but an impurity that clung to him because he was an earthly creature. In the Essenes' wonderful *Hymns of Thanksgiving*, there is a dualism between the spirit and the flesh. The spirit of God is what purifies the elect, and through His supreme and single will and mercy, elevates them above debased human nature.

The spirit worked in them not only at their baptism, but also through their election by God out of the terrible, debased element of humanity.[17] This scheme can be called stratified dualism, a kind of horizontal division beneath which is man as man and above which God in His infinite mercy raises up His elect, the Sons of Light, and gives them His holy, purifying spirit as a free gift.[18] This then, is an approach characteristic of those who feel that there is a corrupt element in man, and it also appears in some important streams in Christianity. The idea of election, which in fact determines that man has no rights, takes a particular form in Christianity, the faith of millions of people.

From a slightly different point of view, one can say that this feeling of repulsion of humanity is one possible way of understanding man. Man sees himself as basically corporeal, and is revolted by his body and its activities. Man even feels a kind of defilement in sexual activity, that "fetid drop" about which the rest of the Jews also speak, which expresses a rejection of natural human existence. This approach is not necessarily a pessimistic one, which leads man to despair. One can distinguish between the power of good, elevation through that sublime element, and the element of flesh itself.

The contrast between spirit and matter was also found among the Greeks, even before the Classical period, in mystical sects and later in certain philosophical schools, particularly in Plato. The Greeks used the term "mind" rather than "spirit." A long time before Plato, this attitude saw the body as a tomb from which the spirit of man, his soul, is liberated at the time of his death. The biblical story in Genesis also speaks of man's being made from clay (*homer* in Hebrew means both "clay" and "matter") of the earth, and it is only the breath of the spirit of life that gave him true life. There is among the Greeks and the Indians, as well as in Buddhism, not only a certain pessimism regarding humanity, but even a general rejection of the material. In this view, man is part of the material world, but part of him is also in the spiritual world; he is part of the world above, the world of the gods.

Here it should be stressed that, while there is certainly the possibility of foreign influence leading the Essenes to adopt the idea of the contrast between flesh and spirit, and perhaps there was even some vaguely influential feeling of crisis and despair at the time when the *Hymns* were written (the reign of Herod, or a little earlier), at the same time there was a great difference between the Greek and the Essene views of the dualism of matter and spirit. The Essenes did not despise this world, and their writings show no rejection of matter in itself. Their loathing was only for the corporeal element in man. God took His elect out of this corporeal element by the gift of the Holy Spirit. And here, again, is another difference: the Essenes did not think that man, in himself, was divided into a corporeal element, which had in it and opposed to it the breath of the spirit of life, but that the entire man, body and soul, existed within the sphere of revulsion, from which one should

54

recoil, while the elect received as a special gift the Holy Spirit (which was not a natural part of the make-up of man). In this way they were redeemed and escaped from the world. The flesh was, then, unredeemed man, and the spirit given to the elect alone was what brought them out of impurity and sin.

These ideas sound familiar, and they are certainly well-known for their influence on Christianity. They can perhaps obtain confirmation precisely in the world in which we live today. Today's crises can sometimes lead one to an existential recoil from the nature of life, just as it did in the case of the Essenes, that same fear of sin and violence. But this ideology, found in the *Hymns*, is given a particular form by the idea of the "election of grace," that God chooses His elect by granting them the Holy Spirit.

Despite their belief in predestination, the Essenes did not imagine that man need not be active. A man had to prove his election through his activity. A member of the sect had to prove, to himself and to others, that he had been chosen to be among the elect of righteousness; that he had received the Holy Spirit, and that God had lifted him out of the state of despair which is natural to man. Each person had to prove this through his acts, and certainly, despite everything, the Essenes were stricter in fulfilling the commandments than other Jews, and saw the Pharisees as those who had chosen the easy way. In the Essenes' opinion, everything depended not on a man's beliefs, nor his acts, but on the will of God, and they interpreted their elevation above human nature as the unique and unconditional act of the will of God, who had chosen them, and no others, by predestination.

These ideas passed into the realm of Christianity, and led it to strange conclusions, different from those of the Essenes. Paul and his followers argued that if everything depended only on election by divine grace, then there is no reward for good deeds, and man's good deeds are like a free gift the Christian receives because he has been chosen and elevated above the sins of the flesh.[19]

In their theories of predestination, the dualism that divides people into the Sons of Light and the Sons of Darkness, and the idea of the spirit which elevates the elect of God above the pollution of the flesh, the Essenes gave an answer, true or imaginary, to basic human feelings. This is why they are still so relevant. It can be said that, in their general outlook, their understanding of the world and the nature of man, and of Jewish monotheism and election by the mercy of God, the Essenes not only expressed universal human feelings more clearly than ever before, but also reached new heights of spirituality and thought.

These Essene ideas had a future. The scrolls should not be seen as merely archaeological or linguistic material. It should be understood that we have here a concentrated group of people occupied in the feverish contemplation of ideas which are relevant to all mankind. From the Jewish foundation developed various theories which, for good or ill, answered exactly to the same extent the needs of men even today. In this respect we should be proud of the scrolls, even if they sometimes repeat themselves, not only because these people pushed forward the frontiers of human thought in different directions, which we will perhaps discuss later, but because they are our ancestors. They were Jews who, thanks to the flowering of Judaism in the Second Temple period, succeeded in tackling, perhaps in a rather Utopian manner, basic human problems which are relevant to us as well.

IX.

The Concept of Man and Human History

The Essenes' particular spiritual achievement resulted both from the fact that they were Jews who lived in a period of flowering, in a closed society of the elect of God, and from their observation, however one-sided, of the nature of man. The Essenes saw man as corrupt by nature, and believed that the Holy Spirit, through the election of God, raised up the chosen one from the corruption. Their understanding of the nature of man was sensitive, if one-sided. On one point there is a possible similarity between the Essenes and Greek philosophical schools — the contrast between the spirit and the flesh. The Essenes' basic idea was that the spirit elevated them above the realm of debased human existence. That is the reason why Josephus compares them with the followers of the Greek philosopher Pythagoras (*Antiquities* XV:37).

The Essenes expected that at the End of Days evil would be put right, man would be cleansed from sin through the baptism of the spirit, all his flesh would be refined, and he (the elect, of course) would return to the state that preceded the original sin and regain the honor lost by Adam.[20] The Essenes hoped that evil would be destroyed at the End of Days, and expressed this hope in the verse: "And it will come to pass when the wombs of injustice are closed," that is when all the openings through which evil penetrated the world would be closed, "wickedness will be driven into exile by justice, as the darkness is driven out by light. And as smoke vanished and is no more, so will wickedness also vanish for ever, and

57

justice will be revealed like the sun in the midst of the heavens, and all those who support the mysteries of wrongdoing will be no more, and knowledge will fill the universe and there will be no more folly for ever."[21] These words may sound strange to us, but that is how they wrote in those days.

So, the openings for deceit will be closed, evil will disappear like smoke, and all the wicked, all those who support the mysteries of wrongdoing, will be no more. That is a vision of an ideal future world. It is a surprising fact that there is Essene influence on the prayer said at *Rosh Hashanah* in the benediction "You are holy": "And thus the righteous will behold and rejoice, the upright exalt and the pious rejoice in song, while iniquity will close its mouth, and all wickedness will vanish like smoke, when You will remove the dominion of iniquity from the earth," precisely in the same order as in the Essene passage of a scroll which scholars call the *Book of Secrets*.

The question is: how will it come about that with the closing of all the openings for evil and the blocking of the source of darkness people will become good; how does evil operate in the world? This is explained in the continuation of the passage: "This is what is to come, and the prophecy is true" — that is the words that are spoken now: the vision of the End of Days — "and know from this that it will not turn back again" — these things will come to pass. And then come the important sentences: "Surely all nations hate injustice, and among them it walks; surely from the mouths of all people truth is preached, and is there a language or a tongue that maintains it? Where is the nation that desires to be wronged by a stronger, and who would wish that his wealth be wrested from him in wickedness?" Thus, there is no nation which has not robbed another nation, and at the same time there is no "nation that desires to be wronged by a stronger." Here we have a classic description of the world within which we live, one that expresses the view that man in fact does desire good, but does evil. The reason for this paradox, according to the author, is that evil comes from outside and corrupts man. According to this passage, when evil is destroyed, then we can all be perfectly righteous. These sentences, which it is worth keeping in mind, tell us to what an extent the Essenes assumed that all the violence in the world, and the evil in it, are the consequence of the sinful nature of man and the element of sin within the world.[22]

The Essenes expressed life as they saw it, through their keen observation of what was happening around them, in their commentaries on the Bible. They also condemned the political exploitation of people: the "last priests of Jerusalem," who "piled up the wealth of the nations," were in their eyes testimony to the avarice of those men who were not elect, condemned at the End of Days to eternal damnation.

Their theological ideas, of themselves as the elect, and their view of the world around them, led the Essenes to the belief that humanity is undergoing a process in many stages. The scrolls thus faithfully reflect the history through which they lived. They assumed that they were already living in the last generation. In a way completely different from that of the Bible, they developed a concept which can be called "the history of salvation," of different stages of human history, in which they were participating, in the sense of "the deeds of the fathers as a sign to the sons"; processes which did not unfold toward the good, but in fact toward a terrible conflict that would come at the End of Days in the War of the Sons of Light against the Sons of Darkness, in which the Sons of Light would defeat the Sons of Darkness, and evil would be destroyed forever. They associated this apocalyptic vision of the End of Days in a theoretical way with what was happening around them. They interpreted everything that happened as a sign that they were right. As Utopian politicians, they showed special interest in some particular events in the history of Israel. Thus, in the scrolls so far published, we can see their reactions to events known to us from other sources, in particular Josephus's account of the Second Temple period.

When in the reign of Alexander Jannaeus the Pharisees revolted against him and joined forces with the Syrian king, Demetrius, the Essenes utterly condemned them. The Pharisees' interference and their invitation to an idolatrous king were wrong.[23] The reign of

Queen Alexandra Salome, usually described in positive terms because she was close to the Sages, is utterly condemned by the Essenes in their *Commentary on Nahum.*[24] They saw the acts of Pompey, who in 63 B.C.E. conquered Jerusalem and brought about a terrible national disaster, as a further revelation of the workings of evil in the world. They saw the fall of the Sadducees at the same time as a sign that one day the Pharisees would also fall, and that eventually their own truth would be revealed.[25] Thus one sees their keen, moralistic and very severe attitude toward evil operating in human history.

With regard to the End of Days, I have already referred in previous chapters to the *Scroll of the War of the Sons of Light against the Sons of Darkness*, that wonderful scroll which was so thoroughly explicated by Yigael Yadin. This describes the war as a type of science fiction, as a war of the stars, in which the Sons of Light fight against the Sons of Darkness with all the most modern means of warfare, and defeat them in seven campaigns. Sometimes the Sons of Light win and sometimes they are defeated, according to the will of God and His secret plan, but eventually the Sons of Light win a wonderful victory with the assistance of God, and one morning they see their enemies, the Sons of Darkness, all lying dead in their camp. Again, "the deeds of the fathers serve as a sign for the sons," and the death of the Sons of Darkness is like the death of the Assyrians in the days of Sennacherib, when they all died outside Jerusalem. Thus the enemy will be struck a supernatural blow, by the sword of God, and the Essenes will seize Jerusalem, will cleanse the Temple, and will conquer the entire world.

There is an element of sober thought strangely combined with this messianic madness, mad visions of things that have still not been fulfilled, for the Essenes no longer exist today. I have referred to the conquest of the Temple. The Essenes' attitude was that the Temple of their days was not valid, not only because those who governed it did not follow the current Essene *halakhah*, but because the Temple ought to have looked different. How they thought it ought to have looked is described in the *Temple Scroll*, which we possess.

The *Temple Scroll*, discovered by Yigael Yadin, is the longest of the scrolls, containing the Essene *halakhah* and describing the liturgical year and the correct way to celebrate the festivals, and the correct appearance of the Temple. Just as the *Scroll of the War of the Sons of Light against the Sons of Darkness* is full of military details, so is this scroll full of architectural and structural details.

The *Temple Scroll* describes the Temple as it should have appeared in their own time. As the Temple in Jerusalem was different from their interpretation, it was not accepted by them. The Temple of the Temple Scroll would not be identical with the eschatological, future Temple, which God would build Himself and which would be different from the Temple as they thought it ought to be in their own time. This would be the Temple of the End of Days, not built by human hands.[26]

The Essenes refused to accept their contemporary Temple, not only because they believed that the future Temple would be different, but because the contemporary Temple did not fit their imaginary scheme. This was also one of the reasons why they did not sacrifice offerings in the Temple in Jerusalem, but only sent gifts (Josephus, *Antiquities* XVIII:19). In their opinion, their way of life was a substitute for offerings sacrificed in the Temple, and the scent of incense arose from their good deeds. Or, as Josephus puts it, they did not sacrifice in the Temple, but only sent gifts, and fulfilled the sacrifices through purification.

The scrolls explain for us this detail of the Essenes' relationship with the Temple. There are scholars who believe that they held their own sacrifices at Qumran. I am not certain of this. Anyway, their meals were a kind of act of sacrifice. Josephus, who fills in the gaps in our information from the scrolls, tells us that when they came to a communal meal they felt a kind of holiness, as if they were in the Temple (*Jewish War* II, 129:133). It seems clear that there was a connection between the fact that they did not sacrifice in Jerusalem and the holiness of the Essene meal. There is apparently some Essene influence on the Christian Mass and Eucharist, for there is a great similarity regarding order and significance between the Essene and the Christian Eucharist, with bread preceding wine.[27]

The Essene view of the world enabled them to look at it clearly, although it also had imaginary elements in it. That "sacred madness" was what allowed them to look at reality in a clear light. The real situation within which they lived was not for them the end of the story, but a kind of reflection of a higher, heavenly reality, which began with the creation of the world, when God made the first man to rule the universe, and divided the world into good and evil, until the time of the End of Days, when evil will be vanquished, the Temple will be rebuilt by God himself, and men will be cleansed of guilty sinfulness. This is a complete and clear conception of man and of the various stages of the world, their own particular conception which led them to embrace the apocalyptic view of which we will speak later.

Thus we have before us a complete and fully thought out world, within which clear ideas interconnect, separate, connect again, in such a way that the whole history of mankind, from its beginning at the creation of the world until its end in disaster and destruction, in which only the elect will be saved, is illuminated in a clear light.

X.

The Phenomenon of the Apocalypts

The Dead Sea Scrolls reflect a complete vision of the world, which seems quite contemporary to us, because the period within which these people lived and thought their thoughts was, like our own period, one of crisis. The Essenes thought that the End of Days was approaching and drawing near, and we, or at least many of us, live with the same fear.

The Essene philosophy, its organization, and its abandoning of the dwellings of the men of evil, were among the most noticeable phenomena of a time of crisis. This time of crisis was reflected in Essene thought in a similar way to which it is reflected by other peoples in other periods. The phenomenon of a crisis and the longing to overcome it through faith in the victory of the defeated has appeared many times in human history. We have witnessed it in peoples penetrated by foreign, European cultures. These native peoples also developed a vision of the end and redemption, and belief in a redemption which gave them the strength to rebel. Let me give one example from modern times — the Indian revolt in the United States. The Indians believed that when, with the help of their god, or of their gods, they succeeded in conquering the United States, the whole country would revert to being prairie, there would be no more firearms, they would go back to fighting with bows and arrows, the bison herds would increase, and America would revert to the ideal state that existed before the coming of the white culture.

Phenomena like these have two aspects, brought about by what is today called acculturization, the penetration of an alien culture. There are messianic, apocalyptic movements that have a retrogressive element in them, like those Indians with their bows and arrows and bisons. And there is also the opposite, a "progressive" vision, when the most sophisticated technical advances that the imagination can invent appear in the vision of the end and redemption. Thus the war that is to come described in the *Scroll of the War of the Sons of Light against the Sons of Darkness* is to be fought according to the most sophisticated military techniques. The Sons of Light are organized according to the model of the Roman army, of all things. Thus we have on the one hand very progressive science fiction, and on the other a return to the ten tribes and an attempt to go back to the time before the original sin, the time of Adam. These two aspects, of ultra-conservatism and an attempt to adapt to modern conditions, exist in various messianic movements.

The Essenes, and the other messianic Jewish movements of the same period, are examples of a total process which took place in the Middle East as a consequence of the breaking up of the ancient social framework of the region and its penetration, in two waves, of what could perhaps be called white European culture. For the first time since Alexander of Macedonia and the coming of the Greeks, Antiochus Epiphanes brought about a crisis among the Jews and aroused apocalyptic hopes.[28] (In my opinion, the conflict between Hellenism and the Jews is also reflected in the *Scroll of the War of the Sons of Light against the Sons of Darkness*.)[29] Later, it was Roman imperialism that aroused people's opposition and the desire for vengeance.[30] Those who had been the rivals of the Greeks joined with the local Greeks of the East and dreamed of apocalyptic eschatology. As a small, imaginary consolation, they imagined a victory of Asia over Europe after a great crisis; a miraculous victory which would be beyond history, and in which many unreal, legendary figures would take part.

The unrealistic approach of these movements, including the Essenes, was an expression of the awareness that they could not in fact overcome the assault of the foreign culture and imperialism,

64

because they were not strong enough. And so a kind of "holy fantasy" developed among these people, in which they imagined the heavens helping them, angels accompanying them, and themselves defeating their enemies and changing the world in which they were oppressed.

The Persians believed in perpetual war between light and darkness, and the Essenes were apparently influenced, in some way, by the Persian religion, which proclaimed that in the End of Days the light would conquer and darkness be destroyed. A religion that saw the world as a power struggle between good and evil, with a conviction of the eventual victory of good, like the Persian religion, would tend, after the invasion of Alexander of Macedonia and later after the Roman invasion, to promote opposition to the alien rulers as a clear religious reaction of Utopianism, which gave the people strength to resist. The other religion that tended to develop apocalyptic beliefs as a reaction to foreign domination was Judaism. Messianic movements arose within Judaism, among them the messianic movement of the Essenes. In Judaism, everything is conditioned on the basic structure of the Torah of Israel, which embraces the fundamental belief that all the world was created by God, and yet Jews accept that the hopes which appear in the Torah and the Scriptures have not been fulfilled unto this day, and that the world is not the world of God in its fullest sense. Certainly, a monotheistic faith like this, with its belief in one God, the Prime Cause, is aware that the world is unredeemed and the present state of the Jewish people is not good. But while the "happy ending" is assured, the Jewish faith tends to give rise, in a situation of internal or external crisis, whether political or social, to that vision of the end and redemption which characterized not only the Essenes, but also other similar movements and trends, what is called the "messianic belief."

The Essenes and their books are part of the wide spectrum known as "apocalyptics," the direct revelation of the mysteries of God, in particular the End of Days which is yet to come. They belonged to what can almost be called an international movement, of both Jews and Gentiles, who reacted to the crisis which afflicted local societies following the penetration of European culture in the days of the Greeks and even more so the Romans, with the despair and hope of powerless people who, nevertheless, had imagination, energy and frustrated strength.

Here we touch on a question directly bound up with the scrolls and what is written in them. Precisely because of their awareness of a crisis which they wished to overcome, the people of the scrolls developed, entirely on their own, an understanding of the political events surrounding them, and, as in parallel movements throughout the world, their approach was anti-imperialistic, because their enemy, as they saw it, was foreign imperialism. In the Essene view, the last Hasmonean priests of Jerusalem, those who had in fact destroyed the earlier social structure (which the Essenes considered an ideal one) belonged to those forces of evil which would be destroyed at the End of Days.

The people who are the victims of such crises which generate a vision of eventual redemption, belong to two groups: the first of these is the members of the former aristocracy and those of the priesthood, who are now unemployed and very frustrated. (In Persia, Alexander of Macedonia burned all the Persian sacred books, so they had to be rewritten from memory.) The place of the priests and the aristocrats is taken by others, and so it is the members of the aristocracy who are harmed. And the second group of victims, of course, and the ones who are most badly affected, are the poor. These two elements are united in the scrolls. On the one side were the priests, not merely the priests, but the Zadokites, the descendants of Zadok, the priest who founded the high priesthood in the reign of King Solomon. The priests, and especially the Zadokites, were the most influential group in the sect. The central task of the priest is attested to in both the scrolls and in Josephus. On the other side were the poor, who saw themselves in a terrible situation as a result of the new imperialism, both internal and external.

The founder of the sect, the one whose name we do not know, who is called the Teacher of Righteousness in the scrolls, was a priest to whom one applied the biblical word "poor" in a quotation from the Bible.[31] If one applies the word "poor" to someone, it is clear that he was not exactly a Rothschild. This means that the founder of the sect, the Teacher of Righteousness, who was a priest, united the two elements: on the one hand the priestly element (presumably if he was called the Teacher of Righteousness, he was one of the Zadokite priests (*zedek* is the Hebrew for righteousness), and on the other hand the ideology of poverty. These two elements, as I have stated, were united in the sect both by its hierarchic structure and its attitude to poverty, which led to the development of its community of property. The Essenes not only had an ideology of poverty among themselves; in their eyes poverty was also a religious value. Thus in their minds the poor were associated with the Zadokite priests, in contrast with the new "capitalistic" aristocracy that arose in the aftermath of the Hasmonean revolt.

Such a unity between poverty, community of wealth, revolutionary mood and messianism was not only typical of the Essenes, but also occurred in the movements which arose after the Reformation in the sixteenth and seventeenth centuries, but this is not the place to go into that.

The apocalyptic approach was one of the fundamental elements in the beliefs of the sect, but there is something else that should also be stated: these people who had no chance of victory longed for the End of Days. They needed that direct revelation of the Spirit of God. But this direct revelation disclosed to them not only the nature of the End of Days, but also the secrets of human existence in general, and so the secrets of the whole world as it really is. These two requirements, the End of Days and the nature of the universe, are neatly summed up in the word "Apocalypse," which means the "direct revelation of the mysteries of God." In a period when men despair of reason, they find themselves in an atmosphere in which they want to get their information from holy men, from visions. People like this no longer believe in science and cannot understand its achievements, and develop, even in scientific fields, a method of discovering "scientific" truths by direct divine revelation.

These elements of the eschatology and of history revealed as near its end, and the revelation of the mysteries of the universe are what are called "apocalyptics," and what the sect called the "miraculous secrets of God." Jewish mysticism was derived from Jewish apocalyptics, and the sect had some influence on its beginnings. The members of the sect occupied themselves with both the mysteries of creation and the mysteries of divinity, as well as with the End of Days and asceticism.

These revelations were so important to the sect that it was forbidden for them to transmit them to outsiders. Their doctrine was an esoteric, secret one. We learn this from the Scrolls and from Josephus, who states this explicitly (*Jewish War* II, 141-142).

XI.

Apocalyptic Literature

Among the works discovered at Qumran are commentaries on books on the Prophets and the Psalms, commentaries which scholars usually call *Pesharim* (the word appears in the scrolls themselves).[32] These are not our normal commentaries, and it is not coincidental that it is precisely upon the books of the Prophets that they comment (and the Psalms were also understood as prophecies). They interpreted the words of these books as if they were describing developments in the world of their own days, as if the Scriptures were alluding to present events, and they developed a particular method of interpreting words, of separating one word from another, of understanding a singular as a plural and *vice versa*, in order to extract from the biblical texts everything they had to say about the present or the future. Take the *Commentary on Habakkuk* for instance: the prophet Habakkuk (2:2) says: "that he who reads may read it speedily," an expression which sounds to us like a general statement. But the people of the scrolls interpreted "he who reads" the words of the Prophet as referring to none other than the Teacher of Righteousness, the founder of the sect. While the Prophet was taking down the words of his vision almost mechanically and without understanding what he was writing, "he who reads" will "read speedily" the words of the Prophets and find in them the theme of the End of Days. Let us quote the full passage, *Commentary on Habakkuk* VII, 3-9: "And as for that which He said, 'That he who reads may he read it speedily,' interpreted this concerns the Teacher of Righteousness, to whom God made known all the mysteries of the words of His servants, the Prophets." Earlier in the same page (VII), we have "And God told Habakkuk to write down that which would happen to the final generation, but He did not make known to him (i.e., Habakkuk) when time would come to an end." According to this, the Prophet himself did not know the End of Days. He only took down what was dictated to him from on High; but he alludes in his words to the one who is yet to come, that is the founder of the sect, the Teacher of Righteousness, who is "he who runs" through the words of the Prophets. It is he who interprets them in an inspired way, and thus he is able to know the End of Days which the Prophets did not know. God had revealed to the Teacher of Righteousness, and apparently to other spiritual leaders of the sect, "the mysteries of the words of His servants, the Prophets."

In order to extract from the Prophets "the mysteries of the words of His servants, the Prophets," the Teacher of Righteousness and his successors developed a special method of foretelling what would happen. Habakkuk talks of the Chaldaeans, and they interpreted this as if he was speaking of the Romans. Once again, the same playing, as it were, with secret meanings. This approach is found not only among them, but also in the ancient literature: people being called not by their names, but by epithets. In this way the system of *pesharim* developed, which enables us to some extent to reconstruct the history of the sect and to see how it saw the future it anticipated.

We mentioned in another context the fact that, according to Josephus, the Essenes could foretell the future. According to him, they could do this because of the purity of their lives, because they had special holy books, and because they read the books of the Prophets (*Jewish War* II:159). Josephus hints, therefore, at a spiritual method of interpretation like this, which breaks the rules of grammar and which can be found in the *pesharim*, the sect's commentaries. In the *Antiquities* he also speaks of Judah the Essene, who prophesied the fate of Antigonus, the brother of Aristobulus I, and who taught his pupils to prophesy (*Antiquities*

XIII:311).

The Essene way of understanding what was happening in the sacred history of the last generation and of forecasting the final redemption to come was, therefore, based not only on the direct vision from God, but on sacred texts interpreted not in their plain sense.

In this way the Essenes, and afterwards their heirs, the people of the New Testament, adopted a very important way of interpreting the Bible, typological interpretation, or in the Talmudic expression, "the deeds of the fathers as a sign for the sons" (what the Bible tells us has happened in the past is an allusion to what will happen in the future). This typological interpretation is indirectly expressed in certain places in the words of the Sages, and was a focus of interest for the sect. They bequeathed this method to future generations, even to the Jews of the Middle Ages (who were evidently influenced by the Christian world, which inherited the Essene method of interpretation). In this method there are types and antitypes. What is written in the Bible alludes to something else, which is interpreted by way of what is written in the Bible.

It is important to ask here how these people could see the history of mankind and their own history, both in visions and in interpretations of those words of the Prophets that were accepted not only by the Dead Sea Sect but also by us, as, for instance, in the *Book of Daniel* and in all apocalyptic literature.

The Dead Sea Scrolls have enabled us to understand this apocalyptic literature, which we had until that time known only from translations into various languages. Very important books, like the *Book of Enoch* and others, were not preserved in Hebrew or Aramaic, and came down to us only through the Christian Church. We did not know the historical process through which this literature developed until the discovery of the scrolls.

One very interesting fact which became clear was that what was found at Qumran included the remains of apocryphal books both known and unknown, which deal with the vision of final redemption and which were formerly known only in translation. Apart from these, fragments were found of books which the Church did not preserve and which were previously unknown. Every little fragment found there contributes to an understanding both of the books (which were previously known only through translations, sometimes corrupt ones) and of the process of this literature's development. In the Bible there is only one apocalyptic book, *Daniel*. It is not accidental that *Daniel* is not included among the Prophets (in the Hebrew Bible), but only in the Hagiographa. Its form suggests that it was written only at a later date, during the reign of Antiochus Epiphanes. Other books were also known, although it was not known where they belonged. And now among the scrolls were found fragments of books which are inter-related and were close to the Dead Sea Sect, but are not obviously sectarian ones.

Let me give the names of some of these books: *The Book of Enoch*, which has survived in its entirety only in an Ethiopian translation. This is a compilation of separate works about Enoch, that wonderful Enoch (Gen. 6:22-24) who walked with God and had direct knowledge of the mysteries of God, of nature, of angels and of the End of Days. Now we have the fragments of this book that were found at Qumran, and they tell us that it was written in Aramaic. There was also a *Book of Noah*, the remains of which are also in Ethiopian. This book was written in Hebrew.

In addition, there is also the book generally known as the *Book of Jubilees*, or more precisely, *The Book of the Division of the Times into their Jubilees and Weeks*, as the members of the sect called it,[33] which relates the history of mankind and of Israel, from the creation to the giving of the Torah, with allusions to the End of Days. The chronology in it is according to "jubilees," or eras, one after another. The book was presumed to have been given to Moses after the giving of the Torah. From the fragments found at Qumran, it appears that the *Book of Jubilees* was written in Hebrew.

A third book is the *Testaments of the Twelve Patriarchs*, the last words of the sons of Jacob before their deaths. This book was known in a later Greek version, and now small fragments of it have been found. One of these is the *Testament of Levi*, or as the scrolls say, "the words of Levi, son of Jacob,"[34] which was written in

Aramaic and which deals not only with divine secrets and the End of Days, but, as Levi was the ancestor of the priests, also with rules of the priesthood and of sacrifices. Fragments of it were found a long time ago in the Cairo Genizah, and more recently among the Qumran Scrolls. Similarly, we have one small fragment of the *Testament of Naphtali* in Hebrew, and now fragments of the *Testament of Judah* have also been found. These apparently come from the same stream from which the Dead Sea Sect arose. These fragments have not yet been published.[35]

This is, however, a complete universe of inter-related works, based on the special, individual calendar of the Dead Sea Sect. There was a broad apocalyptic movement, out of which (thanks to the Teacher of Righteousness) the sect coalesced. The books of the broad movement, which constitute a whole spiritual world, were written at the beginning of the Hasmonean period, some of them perhaps even earlier. Each quotes the other; they are inter-related, and the Dead Sea Sect emerged out of this entire universe. *The Damascus Rule*, one of the writings of the sect, says that they were "like blind men and like them that grope their way" until the coming of the Teacher of Righteousness.[36] That is, they lived within a broad framework, until suddenly a great theologian and a great organizer appeared, who created the sect both structurally and theoretically, as regards their philosophy and their emphasis on predestination, and built an entire intellectual system within the broader movement.

Surprisingly, the books of this broader movement have been preserved among the scrolls. Despite the fact that they had coalesced out of this broader stream, the Essenes apparently valued these books as their own basic texts, and therefore kept them.

Some of these books were already widely known, but it is now possible to see where they came from, from what social environment they sprang, and how they relate to each other. It must be said here that we have a series of inter-related works, characterized by the fact that, like the Dead Sea Sect, they deal with apocalyptic matters and with understanding the miraculous mysteries of the world. Among other matters, they deal with the fall of the wicked angels; the original creation of evil; the world of the angels; the world on high — the heavens; and what there is within the seven heavens, or the three higher heavens. They are also concerned with political matters and the apocalyptic expectations.

Later on other books were written, which no longer belonged to the same movement. The mystical side and the political-ascetic side divided, and from the first century B.C.E. onwards these two themes continue, side by side in different books. Some books in fact deal only with mysticism, while there are also apocalyptic books which are entirely political. As already seen, at the beginning there was a movement, where the two aspects, the mystical and the "political," were combined. It is now possible to put in their right place certain books belonging to this movement, and thus not only to learn more of the history of the people of Israel, but also to see how their great current flowed, split into different branches, and reunited in the Jewish vision of the apocalypse and redemption. It is true that this vision was not fully accepted in the world of the Sages, but there is much common ground between them and this apocalyptic vision. It is this movement which has given us the vision of the apocalypse and Jewish mysticism. This wonderful discovery enables us to trace the origins of Jewish mysticism and the kabbalah to the period before the destruction of the Temple, to marvel at this wonderful Jewish creation and to see how our ancestors thought and responded to the world.

This is, then, the vision of the End of Days which has burned within the heart of the Jewish people throughout its history, that extraordinary hope, the first signs of which are already seen in the books of the Bible. This idea, in one form or another, has been the glowing coal in the heart of the people, which has been able to kindle hope and stimulate action, but has also had the ability to lead the people astray, as in the time of the Zealots, to dangerous adventures that are likely to end in disaster.

The same greatness and the same danger are found in the peculiar world of the Dead Sea Scrolls: greatness of spirit and the danger of unrealistic expectations. We must discuss the particular content of apocalyptic vision not only in the scrolls, but also in all the literature close to the scrolls, in order to examine the question of the historical view in apocalyptic literature. This literature's apocalyptic vision derives from its understanding of human history as being built up in stages determined by God, and a division into "jubilees," in which every jubilee, every period in time, has its own character, its own coloring. History is like a chain made up of links. Jewish history is also made up of a chain of links, and is attached to the links of the general historical chain.

In such a system, each period has its own priest and its own kingdom. In fact there are four kingdoms, which follow each other.[37] Thus there is, so to speak, continuity without development. This is not an evolutionary approach containing the concept of progress, for in this view, it is precisely before the end that the worst time will come, troubles of a kind not seen since the beginning of the world. History and its stages have been predetermined, one after another, by God. And after the final crisis (the War of Gog and Magog, or an invasion of monstrous enemies, or according to another fragment among the scrolls, of a terrible and wicked king, who corresponds with the Christian Antichrist),[38] after all this, the final peace will come; men will live a thousand generations, evil will be destroyed, and an ideal world will come about.

Apparently, the people of the scrolls, as well as others, thought that this world would disappear, and a new world would be created, with new heavens and a new earth.[39] But it is difficult to tell how they depicted this. Certainly the World to Come will be identical in its structure to this one, but it will be purified, shining, full of glory; a world that is perfectly good.

XII.

The Hatred Through the Love

In this chapter we will discuss an interesting problem, which concerns not only the Dead Sea Sect, but the whole of mankind and the relations of each person to the other. On reading Josephus, one gets the impression that the Essenes loved other people to an extraordinary degree. He gives an ideal picture of them; he talks of the way guests were greeted and of mutual love between the Essenes, to such an extent that, before the scrolls were discovered, there was a feeling that this was an outstandingly pious group of great humanitarians, like the followers of Tolstoy. I have mentioned Tolstoy deliberately, because his approach is indirectly derived from the Essenes. The scrolls illuminate the development of certain trends in human thought in a new light. There is Essene influence in Tolstoy's writings, though not directly, but through Christianity, through the influence of the Essene movement on Christianity.

How can we understand the fact that this sect, for whom hatred toward the Sons of Darkness was a clear religious commandment, was also the one whose influence encouraged an excess of love for mankind? It can be said that not only Tolstoy but also Mahatma Gandhi, who was influenced by him, were the distant descendants of the Dead Sea Sect. The difficulty is already made plain in the writings of Josephus, for, together with this idealized description of the Essenes as great humanitarians, who love poverty and put great stress on their relations with others, Josephus also writes that the Essenes wish "to wrong none ... and to hate the unjust and fight the

76

battle of the just." (Jewish War II:139). Josephus certainly enjoyed writing these words alluding to what he had learned from the Essenes, ideas expressed in the War of the Sons of Light against the Sons of Darkness. Love on one side, and hatred on the other.

If we examine Gandhi's methods, we see that he used love and non-violence as weapons to fight against the British, weapons for achieving clear-cut political objectives. In this we can recognize in him a grandson, or great-grandson, or great-great-grandson of the Essenes, for there, too, these matters are ambivalent. These ideas contain within them conclusions that lead in two directions. On the one hand, the Essenes believed in dualism: the division into the Sons of Light and the Sons of Darkness, the Sons of Light, the elect of God, on one side and — opposed to them and against whom they will make war — the Sons of Darkness, who earn the loathing of the world. On the other hand, there is an additional element: the element of predestination. God determines everything, and so He determines even the moment when the time will come for vengeance against the wicked.

Here, precisely at this point, one can turn the method upside down and convert it into one of non-violence and non-resistance to evil, for at the moment when one tries to hasten the end, one is in conflict with the sacred principle of predestination. If one declares war before the appointed time, he is interfering with God's plan.

In this imperfect and complicated world, the Essene who hoped for the bloody and terrible vengeance of the War of the Sons of Light against the Sons of Darkness, had to accept the evil within the world as ordained by God. "I will pay no man the reward of evil; I will pursue him with goodness," and I will always await the Day of Judgment.[40] As time went on and the end did not come, the Essenes developed an idea containing an element which seems to us almost Satanic - the conditional love of peace, or, as Lenin defined it, a militant defeatism. One must acknowledge the government, the authorities, the evil that rules the world during the period of the government of Belial; one must accept this evil submissively and behave toward it as a slave toward his master, and must "leave to them wealth and toils of the hand" (I am quoting from the scrolls[41]),

77

and relate to it with the love of hatred, accept it in the spirit of hatred, and submit totally to the wicked authorities.

From this one can see why the Essenes got on so well with Herod. Herod, who was certainly a wicked king in the eyes of the Essenes and of the whole nation, could rely on the Essenes, not only because Menahem the Essene prophesied how many years he would reign, but because Herod understood better than the Essenes themselves that they would do nothing against him, because it was God who would punish the wicked and would wreak his vengeance on them, and it was forbidden for them to hasten the end. We should cling, as the Essenes said in so many words, to the spirit of hatred, to hatred in the spirit of concealment, and should conceal the hatred. Outwardly, we should behave submissively and with non-violence, until the coming of the Day of Wrath. If a person does not act like this, he is interfering with God's plan and is sinning against it. Thus here we already see some motifs of non-violence. The Essenes did not usually take part in wars. The only exception was the war against the Romans, which was apparently identified by some of the Essenes (including John the Essene, who fell near Ascalon) as the eschatological war. I imagine that most of the Essenes said, "This is not our war, for this is not the time. At this time we must treat the evil in the world as something ordained by God." This idea, which crossed over into Christianity, allows for the possibility of submission, with the maintenance of tension and the expectation that sooner or later the day will come.

In my opinion, there is something Satanic in this Essene approach, but Josephus' description of the Essenes displays their other side, in which hatred can turn into real non-violence, and an unconditional non-resistance to evil into all-embracing love.

Should we then draw the conclusion that Josephus - and Philo of Alexandria - describe only the external, ideal side of the Essenes and actually distort the picture in giving the impression that the Essenes were in a way ancient Tolstoyans? The answer is: yes — and no. The Essenes, as we know them now, were clearly not the world's greatest exponents of love of others and of pacifist non-violence. But their beliefs contained the possibility of pacifism and of universal love.

One should not exclude the possibility that there were among the Essenes individuals or groups whose mutual love was extended to include outsiders, when their submission to the world around them lost the sting of hatred in the spirit of concealment. Thus the possibility cannot be ruled out that there were some Essenes who fitted Josephus' distorted picture.

In the writings discovered at Qumran, we have not found the ideal Essenes of Josephus and Philo. If there were Essenes who more or less fitted this picture, one cannot imagine that the leadership of the sect derived much comfort from them. Moreover, there is another paradox: without doubt there were people who were pacifists and full of universal love, who greatly valued poverty, and whose writings have even come down to us, in Greek. In my opinion, though, these were not real Essenes, but on the periphery of the movement. These people rebelled against the Essene doctrine of hatred, and abandoned its sharp dualism and its characteristically strict doctrine of predestination, and in their place developed a very humane and humanistic doctrine of love, one which was open toward the whole House of Israel. Two works of these circles have been preserved: one is the Jewish source of the Christian composition called the *Doctrine of the Twelve Apostles* (or in Greek, *Didache*[42]); the second work, also in Greek, is called the *Testaments of the Twelve Patriarchs* (or the *Testaments of the Sons of Jacob*) containing the last words of the sons of Jacob before their deaths. These two works are very close to one another in spirit, and both are based on Essene philosophy and Essene writings. The Jewish work behind the first six chapters of the *Doctrine of the Twelve Apostles* is close, from a literary point of view, to the third page of the Scroll of the *Community Rule* at Qumran, while the author of the *Testaments of the Sons of Jacob* uses the *Testaments of Levi, Naphtali* and *Judah*, fragments of which were found at Qumran, and which were written within that broader movement out of which the Dead Sea Sect coalesced.

The Essenes' hatred and their submission to the outside world were based on the idea of double predestination. Some people are destined to be the elect of God, the Sons of Light, while others were destined to be Sons of Darkness. If the idea of predestination is rejected, new possibilities open up. Love, for the orthodox Essene, was possible only among members of the sect. Members were ordered to love their fellows, the Sons of Light, with an absolute love, and secretly to hate the outside world, and to abandon everything to it until the coming of the Day of Judgment, for which they were always ready. If one rejects the attitude that everything is determined beforehand and rejects predestination, it is possible to extend love to everyone. The Essene says, "I will pursue a man with goodness" (*Community Rule* X:19; see also Paul, *Rom.* 12:21), which means that doing good is, in fact, something aggressive, but as soon as one breaks down the strict, closed framework of this sectarian theology, it becomes possible to say that if one relates to the wicked with goodness, he will change his ways and become good. Then the phrase "I will pursue a man with goodness" acquires a new, positive sense. This is possible only if one does not believe that the wicked have been condemned to be wicked before the Creation and cannot change their wickedness. By softening this sort of approach, one reaches the conclusion that it is possible to defeat the wicked by doing good to them, with the result that they will change their ways and become good. Thus we read in the *Testament of Benjamin* (II, 2-3): "The good man has no evil eye, for he has mercy on all, even if they sin. And even if people have evil plots against him, he conquers evil by good..."

Among the *Testaments of the Twelve Patriarchs*, the *Testament of Asher* is an exception. In contrast to the rest of the Testaments, which are full of love for all creation, the *Testament of Asher* breaths a spirit of hatred even more strongly dualistic than the Essene writings at Qumran. In order to explain the difference between the *Testament of Asher* and other Testaments, two approaches are possible, which are not mutually contradictory. It is probable that the Greek *Testament of Asher* was written by a later author than the author who wrote the rest of the *Testaments of the Sons of Jacob*. Moreover, it appears that there was once a *Testament of Asher* in Hebrew or Aramaic, which the Greek author used, and where the dualistic Godhead appeared without later mitigation. In any event, the *Testament of Asher* expresses an extreme hatred of the wicked. As do the rest of the Testaments and the Sages, the *Testament of Asher* also speaks of the two inclinations, inclinations for good and for evil, something which does not appear in the Essene writings at Qumran. According to the Essenes, a person belonged to the light - or to the darkness. On this point the *Testament of Asher* is close to the rest of the Testaments (and different from the Essene doctrine). Moreover, the demonic hatred of evil is more prominent in the *Testament of Asher* than in the scrolls. In this short work, to have mercy on the wicked is certainly a good thing, as far as the feelings of mercy are concerned, but the end tends to evil, while on the other hand to hate the wicked is actually a good thing, although hatred itself is wrong. Thus there is here a kind of dialectic of dualistic hatred (see *Test. Asher*, chapters 2-4).

The *Testament of Asher* is in contrast to the rest of the *Testaments of the Sons of Jacob*, which proclaim undivided love toward the rest of mankind. One should love both the righteous and the wicked! If you love the wicked, you will bring him to repentance and overcome him by doing good to him. It is clear that this Essene periphery was influenced by the universalist doctrine of love of the Pharisee school of Hillel. The circles within which were written the *Testaments of the Sons of Jacob* and the Jewish source of the first six chapters of this *Doctrine of the Twelve Apostles* were of very great importance, for it appears that Jesus was influenced not only by the spiritual world of the Sages, but also by the philosophy of this Essene periphery which, if I am not mistaken, was situated at the point where the left wing of the school of Hillel met the right wing of the Essene movement. There is no doubt that the Essene leadership was opposed to the doctrine of universal love preached by the Essene periphery.

As I mentioned, the *Testaments of the Twelve Patriarchs* express the view that if one did good to the wicked, they would become good. In the Essene view this was impossible, because of the dualism that divided of the world into two camps.[43] The authors of these works, which were produced by people close to the Essenes, pursued Essene ideas in a different direction. They asserted not only non-violence and submission, but also a positive attitude to everybody, even toward the wicked.

When Jesus said that one should not oppose evil, every Essene would agree, but when Jesus preached love toward those who hate one, and associated with prostitutes and tax collectors, the Essene would have raised his voice in protest. The Christians later thought that they could change the world through unbounded love. The Essene would certainly have argued that this was impossible. But within the Essene resignation and belief in predestination the possibility existed of a more positive approach, even one of complete love of others. This approach could come into being out of a combination of the ideas of the pious Pharisees and of the heretical Essenes, an approach which is expressed in the *Testaments of the Twelve Patriarchs*, Greek works which are close to the Essenes and close to the approach of Jesus, and the six Jewish chapters of the *Doctrine of the Twelve Apostles*.

I do not want to say much about our age. In our world, Christian love sometimes wears it Essene form, in which it loves the wicked and hates the righteous. Christian universal love, the origins of which are Essene hatred, can also express a desire for conquest. We have seen this not only in the history of the Church, but also in the approach of the Hindu Gandhi. Even within this reversal, when the dams are burst and universal love is created, this new approach also has an element within it of the desire for mastery over others. The beliefs and the ideas created by the Essenes have influenced the entire world, and thus many of those who proclaim their belief in universal love wish to conquer the world through love.

XIII.

Belief In Messiahs

The Christian belief in the Messiah and the development of similar beliefs among the Jews have led many Jews to confuse belief in redemption and the End of Days with belief in the Messiah, the Son of David. I do not know what will happen in the future, but the belief in an actual Messiah, in the figure of the Messiah, the Son of David, is only one expression of hope for the End of Days, and a new, better world. When one speaks of messianic movements, it would be better to speak of movements concerned with the End of Days, in which the Messiah only represents the desire for redemption. Incidentally, the Essenes for some reason did not like the word ge'ulah for "redemption." The Hebrew root g'al does not appear in the sectarian scrolls at all.[44] If one examines the Jewish faith and its hope for the End of Days, it can be seen that there are books from the Second Temple period in which there is a strong belief in redemption, but the Messiah or, apparently, messiahs, do not appear in them. For instance, one can mention the *Book of Daniel*. It is true that there are messianic symbols in it, but there is no clear-cut belief in an actual messiah. Redemption is what we need, not personalities. In fact, there is no cult of personalities in Judaism, but the troubles that Roman dominion brought on the world led the Sages to develop a hope for a king, a messiah of the House of David, who would lead the nation into battle against the great enemy, the fourth kingdom, Rome. (This is not to say that there was no hope for a single, royal messiah before the Roman period, but at that time it became central to Jewish belief.) The Jewish belief in one or more messiahs is far from complicated. We already read in the *Book of Zachariah* (4:12-14) of the two anointed ones, the Messiah of the House of David, Zerubabel, and the Messiah who is the Priest of the End of Days. This sort of belief was also that of Bar Kokhba. On the coins minted by Bar Kokhba, Shimon (Bar Kokhba himself) appears on one side, while the other shows the priest Eleazar. The priest who ruled Israel from the return from Babylon for a long time was the concrete representative of the regime, and was of decisive importance in the Second Temple period. Thus, as appears from the *Book of Zachariah*, the hope had already arisen in the Persian period that a high priest would stand beside the Messiah of the House of David. The Messiah of the House of David and the Priest were, therefore, important elements in Judaism. They were stressed by the Dead Sea Sect, which emphasized the importance of the Messiahs of Aaron and Israel. The Messiah of Aaron was the Priest. The Messiah of Israel, also called the President of the Community, was the Messiah of the House of David, the Shoot of David, who would sit together with the Priest. In its belief in two messiahs, the Dead Sea Sect was not exceptional, but it emphasized them more than the literature of the Sages does. But because liberation from Rome was so important, the Messiah of the House of David became commonly more important. He was *the* Messiah of Judaism.

The two messiahs were also stressed by the Dead Sea Sect because of the importance they attached to the priesthood. In the earlier chapters I emphasized the priestly element, and the Teacher of Righteousness was himself a priest of the House of Zadok. For this reason the Essenes attached the highest importance to the priestly element, and it is, therefore, not surprising that among the Essenes, and apparently, also within the broader movement out of which the sect coalesced, the Messiah of the Stock of Aaron was of greater importance than the Messiah of the House of David.

Presumably the sect already had its own candidates for this priestly messiah. At one time it evidently thought that the Teacher of Righteousness would be revealed as the Messiah of Aaron. At any rate there are hints at the idea that his successor, the preacher and priest who led the Dead Sea Sect into exile in Damascus, would be revealed as this messiah. It is a very reasonable assumption that this preacher was the son, or another relative, of the Teacher of Righteousness. The Essenes therefore had leaders who could have declared themselves as the Messiah at the right time. The difficulty they faced was a simple one: according to the system already reflected in the *Book of Zachariah*, the Messiah of Aaron, the priestly messiah, could assume his office only when the Messiah of Israel, the Messiah of the House of David, appeared. And he was not to be found.[45] From all this we can draw the conclusion that the Messiah of Aaron, the priestly messiah, was of particular importance to the Dead Sea Sect. This is expressed not only in the scrolls, but also in the works preserved at Qumran which belong to the broader movement out of which the Sect of the scrolls coalesced.

In speaking of the Biblical period, as does the *Book of Jubilees* on the Genesis period, these works speak of Judah and Levi: Judah, the ancestor of David, from whom would come the Messiah of the House of David, and Levi, the ancestor of Aaron, from whom would come the Priest of the End of Days. The *Book of Jubilees*, which is close in outlook to the Essenes, certainly says that Levi is more important than Judah, but does not actually speak specifically about the two messiahs.

One of the scrolls, the *Testament of Levi*, does say specifically: "The priesthood is greater than the kingship." In that case, the differences between this and the faith of the rest of Israel are: a) the scrolls and related works stress the fact that there are two messiahs; b) the difference is a fundamental one, with the emphasis on the importance of the priestly Messiah of the House of Levi as against the Davidic Messiah of the House of Judah.

The ideas are expressed in a fragment of a scroll, *the Testament of Levi* from Qumran. The *Testament of Naphthali*, which expresses the sectarian idea, says that Levi (the ancestor of the Messiah of Aaron), relates to Judah (the ancestor of the House of David), as the sun is to the moon (*Test. Naphthali*, chapter 5).

85

It is precisely this point in the *Testament of Naphthali*, the superiority of the priest over the king, that through an involved process of indirect transmission became a factor in the wars in the Middle Ages between the Papacy, the priesthood as it were, and the Empire, the kingship. One of the Greek manuscripts of the *Testaments of the Twelve Patriarchs*, fortunately for us the best one, was translated from Greek into Latin in England during the papacy of Innocent III, since at that time most people in the West could read only Latin and few knew Greek. The English translator, Robert Grosseteste, translated among the rest of the Testaments also the *Testament of Naphthali*, and it is no coincidence that a few years later the supremacy of Levi over Judah, the priest over the king, served as an argument in the quarrel between the papacy and the monarchy. The papacy was regarded as the priesthood, although admittedly not of the House of Levi, and the monarch, the emperors of the period, as the successors of David. And indeed people soon developed the idea that the Pope was superior to the emperor as the sun is to the moon. As they knew a little more astronomy, they said that all the emperor's power, like the moon's light, came from the light of the Pope, the priest who was the sun. Thus very quickly, within only a few years, these ideas influenced the world at large. But there is a problem: the translator of the *Testament of Naphthali* was born in about 1175, and the Pope used the metaphors of the sun an the moon with reference to the papacy and the monarchy in a letter of 1198. So, did the translation already exist?

And that is not the end of the story. Dante, whom we know for the *Divine Comedy*, supported the emperors against the Popes. In his work on monarchy, which was banned by the Church, he wrote (Book III, chapters 4—5) that those who argued that the Papacy was superior to the monarchy because Levi was born before Judah were wrong because, according to their logic, says Dante, the beasts would be superior to man, because they were created before Adam. (The idea that Levi was superior to Judah because he was born first is not found in the *Testaments of the Sons of Jacob*.)

It should also be noted that in the system developed by the sect there was also a third figure, based on ideas of the Second Temple period. In one place in an Essene work it states that all these things would continue until the coming of the Prophet and the Messiahs of Aaron and Israel (*Community Rule* IX:11). Thus apart from the two messiahs, the Prophet of the End of Days must also come.[46] Like all of Israel, the members of the sect started from the assumption that prophecy had ceased and that at the End of Days, therefore, a prophet would come who could be (in the rabbinic sources) identified with the Prophet Elijah, or in other sorces who was sometimes just called the "Prophet," who would renew the prophecy that had ceased. The term was taken from Deut. 18:19, a word which became important both in Christianity (the prophet Jesus) and in Islam (the prophet Mohammed).

According to *Maccabees* I (4:44—46), at the time of the dedication of the Temple by Judah the Maccabee, they did not know what to do with the stones of the altar that had been defiled. So they put them away, until the coming of a prophet who could decide. In the same book (14:41) it is written in the "declaration of independence" presented to Shimon, the brother of Judah the Maccabee, that "the Jews and the priests decided that Shimon would be priest and ruler for ever, until a true prophet should arise." Thus we already see here the three roles which, according to the Dead Sea Sect, will all (not only the Prophet, as it says in this "declaration of independence") be filled by three separate people at the End of Days. "Until the coming of the Prophet and the Messiahs of Aaron and Israel." The Essene belief was, therefore, the hope for three 'Redeemers" and the expectation of the End of Days, while among the Hasmoneans the development was in the opposite direction: the three crowns were to be united in one man in their own time.

In the court of Shimon's son, John Hyrcanus, he had some supporters who claimed that the condition of the prophet who had yet to come had been cancelled and that the rule of the Hasmonean house was no longer a temporary one: John, the priest of the Supreme God, who was blessed with the prophetic gift, united in his person the three crowns of kingship, priesthood and prophecy (Josephus, *Jewish War* I:69; *Antiquities* XII:300). The idea of the three crowns was, therefore, not an Essene invention, but for them not only the Prophet, but also the true priest, the Priest of Righteousness, and the Messiah of the House of David were still to come in the future. In one of the scrolls, the Prophet of the End of Days is called "the Messiah of the Spirit"[47] — he would become a messiah through a Holy Spirit. Later there were Christians who believed that the three roles had been united in Jesus of Nazareth. This is not the place to dwell on this point, although it is at least interesting to note that the Essene doctrine of the three messiahs indirectly influenced the Christian dogmatics of Calvin. The threefold division of Christ's role as priest, king and prophet became the basis for a large part of the Calvinist system.

Let us return to the subject of the cessation of prophecy in Israel and the longing for its renewal. We have already seen that the cessation of prophecy troubled not only the Hasmoneans and their followers (as we learned from *Maccabees* I), but also the Essenes. The concern of the latter, which gave rise to the hope for the coming of a prophet, is a little surprising, not only because many prophetic and visionary works were written within the broader apocalyptic movement out of which the Essene sect emerged, but because even the Essenes themselves were known as prophets of the future. And in general, the prevailing atmosphere among the Essenes was one filled with the spirit of prophecy. The sect's commentaries on the prophetic books demonstrate the great honor in which the Essenes held biblical prophecy. They defined their studies as "the study of the Law which He commanded by the hand of Moses, that they may do according to all that has been revealed from age to age, and as the Prophets have revealed by His Holy Spirit" (*Community Rule* VIII:15—16; compare also I:3). In contrast, the Pharisee Sages saw the Torah of Moses (and the Oral Law) as the basic element. The Essenes, therefore, argued against the Pharisees that "They have thrown behind their backs all His commandments that He had delivered unto them by the hand of the Prophets, and they listened to their seducers and honored them... and they feared them as gods in their blindness."[48]

Despite the prophetic atmosphere among them, the Essenes

evidently did not consider themselves of equal rank with the biblical Prophets. They never refer to themselves prophets; they speak of visionaries, but not of prophets, and look forward to the coming of the true Prophet at the End of Days.

Other messianic beliefs also developed around the Dead Sea Sect. Some people believed in the coming of a superhuman creature called the "Son of Man" (thus in the *Book of Enoch*) and in that wonderful figure, the Judge of the End of Days, identified in one of the Scroll fragments with Melchizedek, the King of Salem, who is not dead, but will sit at the right hand of God at the End of Days.[49] Here too are the echoes of what was to come. The Dead Sea Sect, like the rest of the House of Israel, also believed in actual messiahs, but this belief was not so important for them as the belief in salvation and the End of Days. Here we can see the great variety of beliefs in concrete messiahs, and of ideas of redemption in general.

The Essenes' longing was not satisfied, but it fertilized human history, as did the other ideas of the Dead Sea Sect. This longing, which gave them the strength to endure torture and suffering and to create a society which can serve as an example even in the present day, beats in our hearts too. But what we, in contrast to the Essenes and other similar messianic movements, must do is not speak of all this, but think about it. Ther words were said by a wise man[50] on another subject: we must not let these hopes rule our lives, or revive mythological or mystical motifs. We must hope for salvation, but live in this world as it is.

The Spiritual History of the Dead Sea Sect

NOTES

(N.B. Wherever possible, quotations from the Dead Sea Scrolls, both in the text and in the notes, are taken from the version of G. Vermes, *The Dead Sea Scrolls in English*, Penguin Books, Harmondsworth, 1965.)

1. A detailed discussion of the ancient sources of the Essenes can be found in E. Schürer, *The History of the Jewish People in the Age of Jesus Christ* Vol II, ed. F.B.G. Millar, G. Vermes and M. Black (Edinburgh, 1979), pp. 555-590.
2. On the name "Essenes" and suggested interpretations, see Schürer, pp. 559-560.
3. On this see, in particular, J. Licht, "The Plant Eternal and the Temple of Divine Deliverance, Essays on the Dead Sea Scrolls," (Jerusalem, 1961), pp. 49-75 (Hebrew).
4. On this see D. Flusser, "Jerusalem in the Literature of the Second Temple," *Ve'im Bigevurot, Essays Presented to Reuben and Hannah Mass* (Jerusalem 1974), pp. 268-273 (Hebrew).
5. See D. Flusser, "Pharisees, Sadducees and Essenes in Pesher Nahum," *Sefer Zikharon li-Gedaliyah Alon* (Tel Aviv 1970), pp. 133-168 (Hebrew); in German: "Pharisaer, Dadduzaer und Esseuer in Pescher Nahum," Qumran, 1981, pp. 121-166.
On the Essene opposition to Rome, see D. Flusser, "The Roman Empire as Seen by the Hasmoneans and the Essenes," *Zion* 48 (Jerusalem 1983), pp. 149-176 (Hebrew).
6. See previous note.
7. The Masoretic text reads: "And he warned me not to follow," or "and instructed me that I should not walk," but another vocalization of the Hebrew would give us the version "and he turned me...," which is attested by a number of Greek versions, as well as the Dead Sea Scroll of Isaiah. See also my article cited in note 4 above, p. 271.
8. The word *hasidim* does appear in the hymns found at Qumran, but these hymns do not display clear signs of Essene terminology, nor of the sect's outlook.
9. An outstanding example is "But Thou, O my God, hast succored the soul of the poor and the needy against one stronger than He;" (*Hymns* II, 34-35 (Vermes, 3:14-16, p. 156)), based on *Jeremiah* 31:10, where the verb "redeem" (*ga'al*) appears in the Hebrew text.
10. See *Hymns* IV, 7-12 (Vermes 7:6-22, p. 61):
    Teachers of lies [have smoothed] Thy people [with words],
    and [false prophets] have led them astray;
    They perish without understanding
    for their words are in folly.
    For I am despised by them
    and they have no esteem for me
    that Thou mayest manifest Thy might through me.
    They have banished me from my land
    like a bird from its nest;

all my friends and brethern are driven far from me
and hold me for a broken vessel.
And they, teachers of lies and seers of falsehood,
have schemed against me a devilish scheme,
to exchange the Law engraved on my heart by Thee
for the smooth things (which they speak) to Thy people.
And they withhold from the thirsty the drink of Knowledge,
and assuage their thirst with vinegar...

11. The passage that refers to it is the *Commentary on Habakkuk* XI:4-8 (Vermes, p. 241): "...the Wicked Priest who pursued the Teacher of Righteousness to the house of his exile, that he might confuse him with his venomous fury. And at the time appointed for rest, for the Day of Atonement, he appeared before them to confuse them, and to cause them to stumble on the Day of Fasting, their Sabbath of repose."

12. Josephus, *Antiquities* XIII::172: "But the sect of the Essenes affirms that fate governs all things, and that nothing befalls men but what is according to its determination." (Translation by W. Whiston, *The Works of Flavius Josephus* (Edinburgh, undated.) A parallel is to be found in the *Community Rule* 3:15-16 (Vermes, p. 75): "From the God of Knowledge comes all that is and shall be. Before ever they existed He established their whole design, and when, as ordained for them, they cone into being, it is in accord with His glorious design that they accomplish their task. The laws of all things are unchanging..."

13. E. Meyer, *Ursprung und Anfaenge des Christientums* Vol. II (1921), p. 402.

14. This is the passage that reveals the cracks in the Essene system, *Community Rule* 13:18-25 (Vermes, pp. 75-6):
He has created man to govern the world, and has appointed for him two spirits in which to walk until the time of His visitation: the spirits of truth and falsehood. Those born of truth spring from a fountain of light, but those born of falsehood spring from a source of darkness. All the children of righteousness are ruled by the Prince of Light and walk in the ways of light, but all the children of falsehood are ruled by the Angel of Darkness and walk in the ways of darkness.
The Angel of Darkness leads all the children of righteousness astray, and until his end, all their sin, iniquities, wickedness, and all their unlawful deeds are caused by his dominion in accordance with the mysteries of God. Every one of their chastisements, and every one of the seasons of their distress, shall be brought about by the rule of his persecution; for all his allotted spirits seek the overthrow of the sons of light.
But the God of Israel and His Angel of Truth will succor all the sons of light.

15. This dualism is defined in, among other places, *Community Rule* 3:25 - 4:1 (Vermes, p. 76), in the following words: "For it is He who created the spirits of Light and Darkness and founded every action upon them and established every deed [upon] their [ways]. And He loves the one everlastingly and delights in its works for ever; but the counsel of the other He loathes and for ever hates its ways."
Compare also:
The nature of all the children of men is ruled by these (two spirits), and

during their life all the hosts of men have a portion in their divisions and walk in (both) their ways. And the whole reward for their deeds shall be, for everlasting ages, according to whether each man's portion in their two divisions is great or small. For God has established the two spirits in equal measure until the final age, and has set everlasting hatred between their divisions. Truth abhors the works of falsehood, and falsehood hates all the ways of truth. And their struggle is fierce for they do not walk together.

16. *Hymns* 4:29-30 (Vermes, p. 163):
What is a creature of clay
for such great marvels to be done,
whereas he is in iniquity from the womb
and in guilty unfaithfulness until his old age?

17. Here I shall cite the entire passage, *Hymns* 4:29-33 (Vermes, pp. 163-4), part of which I cited in the last note. The passage should be considered as a classic expression of Jewish thought.
But what is flesh (to the worthy) of this?
What is a creature of clay
For such great marvels to be done,
whereas he is in iniquity from the womb
and in guilty unfaithfulness until his old age?
Righteousness, I know, is not of man,
nor is perfection of way of the son of man:
to the Most High God belong all righteous deeds.
The way of man is not established
except by the spirit which God created for him
to make perfect a way for the children of men.
that all His creatures might know
the might of His power,
and the abundance of His mercies
toward all the sons of His grace.
This passage, or one similar to it, was known to the author of the Judeo-Greek work *The Wisdom of Solomon* (9:13—18).

18. It is instructive that the phrase "Sons of Light" is not found in the *Hymns*, just as the name Belial, which in other places indicates the leader of the forces of evil, loses its personal aspect in the *Hymns*, and becomes simply a term for evil.

19. The phrase "sin in the flesh" is found in the *Community Rule* (XI:2), as well as in Greek in the New Testament (Paul, *Romans* 8:3).

20. I shall quote the following passage in full, *Community Rule* IV:18-23 (Vermes, pp. 77-78):
But in the mysteries of His understanding, and in His glorious wisdom, God has ordained an end for falsehood, and at the time of the visitation He will destroy it for ever. Then truth, which has wallowed in the ways of wickedness during the dominion of falsehood until the appointed time of judgment, shall arise in the world for ever. God will then purify every deed of man with his truth; He will refine for Himself the human frame by rooting out all spirit of falsehood from the bounds of his flesh. He will cleanse him of all wicked deeds with the spirit of holiness; like purifying waters He will shed upon him the spirit of truth (to cleanse him) of all abomination and falsehood. And he shall be plunged into the spirit of

purification that he may instruct the upright in the knowledge of the Most High and teach the wisdom of the sons of heaven to the perfect of way. For God has chosen them for an everlasting Covenant and all the glory of Adam shall be theirs. There shall be no more lies and all the works of falsehood shall be put to shame.

21. These words are from a work which scholars call the *Book of Secrets*, of which only fragments were found among the scrolls. The passage discussed was republished by J. Licht, *Megilat ha-Hodayot* (Jerusalem), p. 242.

22. At the same time, the passage which has been preserved of the Essene *Book of Secrets* is not characteristic of Essene belief in the dualism of good and evil, since according to this passage it appears that the nature of *every* man is good. The philosophy of this passage, and even its style, is more reminiscent of the philosophy of the Stoic school. Compare also Paul's *Epistle to the Romans* 7:14-25.

23. The *Commentary on Nahum* I:2 (Vermes, p. 231) speaks of "Demetrius, king of Greece who sought, on the counsel of those who seek smooth things, to enter Jerusalem." On this incident, see Josephus, *Antiquities* XII:377-386.

24. The ascendancy of the Pharisees during the reign of Queen Alexandra Salome is described in the *Commentary on Nahum* II:2-10 (Vermes, p. 233), which speaks of:

    Those who smooth things... Captivity, looting and burning shall be among them, and exile from dread of the enemy... those who lead Ephraim astray, who lead many astray through their lying tongue, and deceitful lips – kings, princes, priests and people, together with the stranger who joins them. Cities and families shall perish through their counsel; honorable men and rulers shall fall through their tongue's [decision].

25. On the future revelation of the truth of the Essenes' faith and of its expected consequences, see *Commentary on Nahum* III:2-5 (Vermes, p. 233).

    Interpreted, this concerns those who seek smooth things, whose evil deeds shall be uncovered to all Israel at the end of time. Many shall understand their iniquity and treat them with contempt because of their guilty presumption. When the glory of Judah shall arise, the simple of Ephraim shall flee from their assembly; they shall abandon those who led them astray and shall join Israel.

    1On the fall of the Sadducees at the time of Pompey and on the Essenes' hope that the Pharisees would also fall in the future, see *Commentary on Nahum* IV:3-6 (Vermes, p. 234):

    Interpreted, this concerns Manasseh [i.e., the Sadducees] in the final age, whose kingdom shall be brought low by sword. His wives, his children, and his little ones shall go into captivity. His mighty men and honorable men [shall perish] by the sword... the wicked of Ephraim [i.e. the Pharisees]... whose cup shall come after Manasseh.

26. And thus God is made to say in the *Temple Scroll* 29:7-10:

    And I shall accept them and they shall be My people, and I shall be for them for ever. I will dwell with them for ever and ever and will sanctify My sanctuary by My glory. I will cause My glory to rest on it until the day of creation on which I will create My sanctuary, establishing it for myself for all time according to the covenant I have made with Jacob in Bethel.

    Compare also *Book of Jubilees* I:26; IV:26.

27. It is well known that the usual order of the Jewish meal is first wine and then

bread, and this is how Jesus conducted the Last Supper. The order of the Essene meal was first bread and them wine, and this is the order of the Christian meal (the Eucharist) from as early as the time of Paul. See:
D. Flusser, "The Last Supper and the Essenes," *Immanuel*, Jerusalem 1973, pp. 23-27.
D. Flusser, "Die Sakramente und das Judentum," *Judaica*, Basel 1983, pp. 3-7.

28. On the reaction of the Orient to the formation of Greek kingdoms after the conquests of Alexander of Macedonia, see S.K. Eddy, *The King is Dead*, Lincoln 1961. *The Book of Daniel*, the only apocalyptic work included in the Hebrew Bible, was the one Jewish book which, in its final form, was an expression of opposition to the Greek kingdom. One should note here that Jewish (and Gentile) literature written in an apocalyptic strain reflects *only indirectly* opposition toward the invading culture and civilization. Its main interest is in ideological warfare against the imperialism that had invaded the region. Incidentally, the revolt against Antiochus Epiphanes did not originate in the clash between two cultures, as in generally assumed (and, unfortunately, this is not the place to discuss this matter in detail). In *Maccabees* I, Antiochus Epiphanes, his successors and their people are never called Greeks. The problem of the relations between Hellenism and Judaism is a crucial issue in *Maccabees* II, which was written by a Hellenized Jew, and the whole issue needs further research. It is clear that the main issue in the Hasmonean revolt was opposition to the anti-Jewish decrees of the pagan Seleucid kingdom.

29. On this, see: D. Flusser, "Apocalyptic Elements in the War Scroll," *Jerusalem in the Second Temple Period* (Jerusalem 1981), pp. 434-452 (Hebrew). On p. 449 of this article, I proposed supplying in the *Scroll of the War* I, 4—5: "to destroy and to cut off the horn [of Israel]." Meanwhile, my proposal had been confirmed by the publication of another copy of the *Scroll of the War* (4Q 496). The fragment was published in the collection DJD (Oxford 1982), p. 58.

30. On this issue, see in particular my second article cited in note 5 above.

31. *Commentary on Psalm 37*, II, 16-20:
    The wicked draw the sword and bend their bow to bring down the poor and needy and to slay the upright of way. Their sword shall enter their own heart and their bows be broken (14-15). Interpreted, this concerns the wicked of Ephraim and Manasseh, who shall seek to lay hands on the Priest and the men of his Council at the time of trial which shall come upon them. But God will deliver them from out of their hand.
    The Priest, of course, is the Teacher of Righteousness, as is clear in what follows (3,15): "The Priest, the Teacher of Righteousness." It is to him that the words "poor and needy" are applied, and this means that he was not rich. He and his sect were persecuted by "Ephraim and Manasseh," and we have already seen that these are the names used for the Pharisees and Sadducees.

32. This noun also appears once in Hebrew in *Ecclesiastes* 8:1, and in Aramaic in the *Book of Daniel*.

33. *Damascus Rule* XVI:2-4 (Vermes, p. 109): "As for the exact determination of their times to which Israel turns a blind eye, behold it is strictly defined in the *Book of the Division of the Times into their Jubilees and Weeks*." Hence, it is clear that the Essenes relied on the *Book of Jubilees* for their own peculiar

94

calendar.

34. The whole passage, which is reminiscent of the *Testament of Levi*, is found in the *Damascus Rule* IV:14-19 (Vermes, p. 101):

> Interpreted, these are the three nets of Satan with which Levi son of Jacob said that he catches Israel by setting them up as three kinds of righteousness. The first is riches, the second is fornication, and the third is profanation of the Temple. Whoever escapes the first is caught in the second, and whoever saves himself from the second is caught in the third.

Apart from the Aramaic fragments of the *Testament of Levi* found at Qumran, a larger number of fragments of this work were found in the Cairo Genizah. There is no doubt that the work stems from Qumran. These Genizah fragments were recently republished by J.C. Greenfield and M.E. Stone, "Remarks on the Aramaic Testament of Levi from the Geniza," *Revue Biblique* 86, 1979, pp. 214-230. Some passages of the Greek translation of this work were also found in a certain Greek manuscript. For a German translation of all the fragments of the original *Testament of Levi*, see J. Becker, Die *Testamente der XII Patriarchen*, Gutersloh, 1924, pp. 139-151.

35. I assumed the existence of this *Testament of Judah* in my entry dealing with the *Midrash va-Yissa'u* in Encyclopaedia Judaica XI (Jerusalem 1972), pp. 1520-1521. In that case, at least three testaments of the sons of Jacob were written within the movement inside which the Essene community was formed, and fragments of these have been preserved among the scrolls: the *Testament of Levi* (Aramaic), the *Testament of Naphthali* (Hebrew), and the *Testament of Judah* (language so far unknown). The Greek work known as the *Testament of the Sons of Jacob*, or the *Testament of the Patriarchs*, was based on the individual testaments of the sons of Judah. This work has reached us in a slightly Chrsitianized version, but it is essentially a Jewish work composed in circles close to the Essenes, but differing from them in some of its views. See my article in *Encyclopaedia Judaica* XIII (Jerusalem 1972), pp. 184-186. On the Hebrew *Testament of Naphthali*, which is not identical with the one of which a fragment has been preserved among the scrolls and which, despite being close to the Greek testaments, is not a translation from them, see my article in *Encyclopaedia Judaica* (Jerusalem 1972), pp. 821-822.

36. *Damascus Rule* I, 5-11 (Vermes, p. 97):

> And in the age of wrath, three hundred and ninety years after He had given them into the hand of King Nebuchadnezzar of Babylon, He visited them, and He caused a plant root to spring from Israel and Aaron to inherit His Land and to prosper on the good things of His earth. And they perceived their iniquity and recognized that they were guilty men, yet for twenty years they were like blind men groping their way.
>
> And God observed their deeds, that they sought Him with a whole heart, and He raised for them a Teacher of Righteousness to guide them in the way of His heart.

The details of this passage are not always clear to us, but in general it confirms our hypothesis.

37. Despite the importance of the system of the four kingdoms, both among the Talmudic Sages in the *Book of Daniel* (which was also accepted by the Dead Sea Sect), it is interesting that neither the strictly Essene writings, nor the

apocalyptic writings composed within the broader movement to which they belonged, uphold this vision of the four kingdoms. They have a different system of historical stages.

38. The passage concerning the Wicked King at the End of Days, which is the oldest testimony concerning the Antichrist to reach us, is published with a commentary in my article: "The Hubris of Antichrist," *Immanuel* 10 (Jerusalem 1980), pp. 31-37.

39. See the quotation from the *Temple Soul* cited in note 26 above. We also have in *Hymns* XIII:11 (Vermes, p. 191) the expression "and creating new things."

40. Here is the whole passage:

> I will pay to no man the reward of evil;
> I will pursue him with goodness.
> For judgment of all the living is with God
> and it is He who will render to man his reward.
> I will not envy in a spirit of wickedness,
> my soul shall not desire the riches of violence.
> I will not grapple with the men of perdition
> until the Day of Revenge.

(*Community Rule* X:17-19 (Vermes, pp. 90-91))

The expression "I will pursue a man with goodness" has a parallel in Paul's *Epistle to the Romans* 12:21. The whole of that passage (*Romans* 12:9-13, 7) is influenced by Essene attitudes. See my article "A Jewish Source of the Approach of the Early Church to the State," in my *Jewish Sources in Early Christianity*, Sifriat Poalim 1979, pp. 397-401 (Hebrew).

41. The whole of this crucial passage, which teaches the Essene how to adapt himself to the circumstances of his time, while at the same time remaining faithful to the principles of his sect, can be found in *Community Rule* IX:12-24 (Vermes, pp. 87-88). The whole passage repays careful study, but we will cite here only the important parts which touch on the Essenes' aggressive passivity toward their environments:

> These are the precepts in which the Master shall walk in his commerce with all the living, according to the rule proper to every season and according to the worth of every man...
> He shall not rebuke the men of the Pit nor dispute with them.
> He shall conceal the teaching of the Law from men of falsehood,
> but shall impart true knowledge and righteous judgment to those who have chosen the way. He shall guide them all in knowledge according to the spirit of each and according to the rule of the age...
> These are the rules of conduct for the Master in those times with respect to his loving and hating.
> Everlasting hatred in a spirit of secrecy for the men of perdition: He shall leave to them wealth and earnings like a slave to his lord and like a poor man to his master.
> He shall be a man zealous for the Precept whose time is for the Day of Revenge. He shall perform the will of God in all his deeds, and in all his dominion as He has commanded.

Compare also the passage quoted in note 40 above. These passages constitute one of the firmest proofs identifying the Dead Sea Sect with the Essenes, since they are almost tailor-made to explain Josephus' words on the Essenes in *Jewish War* II, 140.

43. On this see D. Flusser, "The Two Ways," *Jewish Sources in Early Christianity*, Sifriat Poalim 1979, pp. 235-252.

The members of the Dead Sea Sect were so extreme in their dualism between the Sons of Light and the Sons of Darkness, that they used to recite in a liturgical way in their ceremonies, among other curses on the men of the lot of Satan: "May God not heed you when you call on Him, not pardon you by blotting out your sin;" (*Community Rule* II:8 (Vermes, p. 73)). In their opinion only the men of the lot of God obtain pardon and remission of sins.

44. See note 9 above and the context of this note.

45. See D. Flusser, "Two Notes on the Midrash on I Sam. VII," *Israel Exploration Journal* 9 (Jerusalem 1959), pp. 99-109.

See also J. Liver, "The Doctrine of the Two Messiahs in Sectarian Literature," *Harvard Theological Review* 52, 1959, pp. 149-185.

46. In the Qumran fragment which scholars call 4Q Test (published in the collection 4DJDV, pp. 57-60) we have three groups of biblical quotations. The first alludes to the Prophet, the second to the King, the third to the priesthood. They are followed by another passage.

47. 11Q Melch, column B, line 18: "The seeker is the Messiah of the Spirit." See P.J. Kobelski, *Melchizedek and Melchiresa*, Washington, 1980, p. 6.

48. *Commentary on Hosea* (4Q 166) 2, 3-6. See the text in M. Horgan, *Pesharim* I, Washington 1979, p. 39.

49. See D. Flusser, "Melchizedek and the Son of Man," *Christian News from Israel*, April 1966, pp. 20-23. The best edition of the text can be found in Kobelski (see note 47 above), pp. 3-23. See also E. Puech, Revue de Qumran, 1987, pp. 483-513. It is clear that this figure of the "Son of Man" was not an invention of the broader movement from which the Essenes emerged, since it appears in other Jewish apocalyptic writings as well. Jesus also expected the arrival of the "Son of Man." On this concept, see D. Flusser, "Jewish Messianic Figures in Early Christianity," *Messianism and Eschatology*, Shazar Center, Jerusalem 1984, pp. 105-113 (Hebrew).

50. The French leader Gambetta after the loss of Alsace-Lorraine in 1870. He stated this in a speech on November 16, 1871. See G. Buchman, *Geflugelte Worte*, Ullstein, 1986, p. 333.